"Secrets for Relational Living"

Written by
Debbye Graafsma, dmcc, bcpc

Awakened to Grow
P.O. Box 546
Indian Trail, NC 28079 704-
562-2897

DISCLAIMER

The lesson materials contained in this handbook are provided for informational purposes only. These materials, and any or all accompanying materials published by the author, are not in any way intended to diagnose, treat, or evaluate mental illness; nor are they a substitute for professional counseling and care. Those who suffer from the difficulties covered in "A Christian Counselor's Primer On ..." series of booklets should seek additional counsel for their unique situation. Optimally, the materials should be worked through with a trained professional counselor.

The information contained herein is provided for educational purposes only. The user assumes all risks. Debbye Graafsma, Awakened to Grow, and their affiliates deny responsibility for any and all misuses of the information provided.

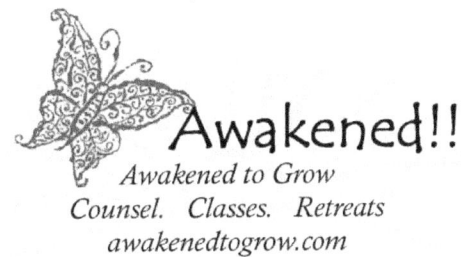

Awakened to Grow Ministries
P.O. Box 546
Indian Trail, NC 28079
Website: awakenedtogrow.com

All materials, charts, artwork and concepts are copyrighted with all rights reserved.

© 2011 Debbye Graafsma, Awakened to Grow.
ISBN -- 978-0-9852680-5-3

No duplication may be made without prior written consent from the author/publisher.
Thank you for your integrity.

Secrets for Relational Living

What you will gain from this class:

"Secrets for Relational Living" is designed to help the student discover where they are presently living in the skill-set of living in their ability to relate well to other people, and to provide an essential tool-box for growth, discovery and development. The class journey begins with the foundational understanding of God's plan for His Creation to live in relationship. We will then define the characteristics of healthy bonding and attachments, first from God's viewpoint, and then from a human standpoint. The student will be given the opportunity to assess past and present behavior patterns in how they approach and address relationships, taking a short period to delve into the "why's" of behavior patterns. From there, the class materials will provide the student with discovery materials to learn new patterns, providing the opportunity for growth and personal development, in spiritual discipleship and in human relationship.

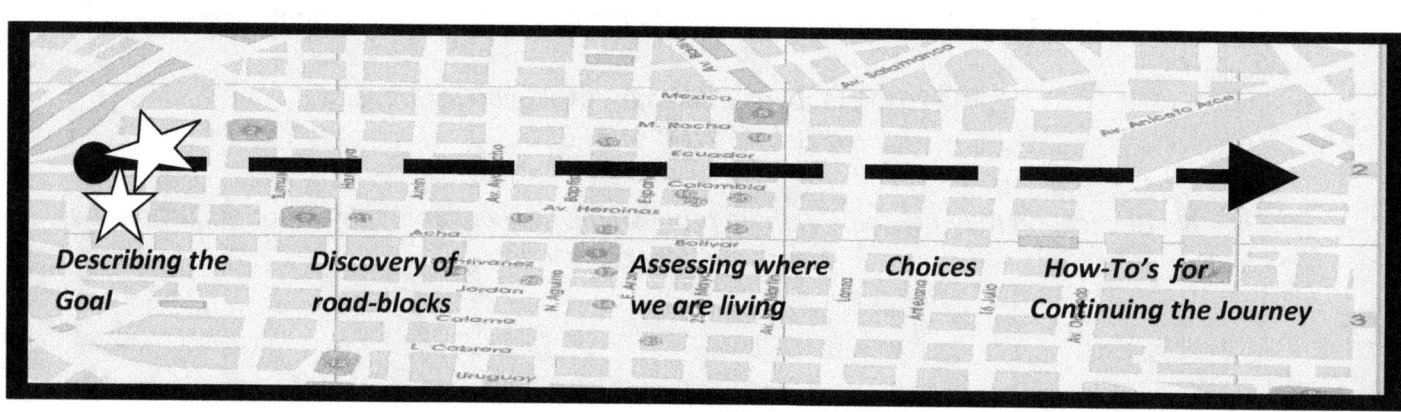

Session One—"The Original Design"

What we will learn in this Session:

We were created for the purpose of relationship; first with God, and then with others. So, in learning the process of how healthy relationships happen, it becomes necessary to study the Creator's original design and plan for relationship. We will learn God's design for relationship, how that relationship was broken and distorted, and how to begin the process of restoration.

The Instructor's Goal for this Session:

To partner with the student, enabling them to begin with correct theology regarding the process and purpose of relational living.

Session One—"The Original Design"

(Genesis 1-3)

What is relational living? What were we designed to do in the first place?

Introduction and Class Premise:

"In the Beginning..."

1. Adam understood God; God understood Adam. There was moment by moment communication between them. Adam was a spiritual being. (Genesis 2:7)

2. Adam understood and embraced who he was.
He had been formed in the likeness of his Creator. (Genesis 1:27)

3. **Adam was originally male and female in one being.**
(Genesis 1:26 and Genesis 2:18-25)

4. Adam *(male and female)* **had a purpose.** (Genesis 1:28)

1. Adam was to _subdue_ the earth ("kavash" (Heb) -- bring into subservience) the earth.

2. Adam was to _fill_ the earth with descendants. ("mala" (Heb) – to fill and satisfy)

3. Adam was to _rule_ over everything on the earth ("radah" (Heb) – to have dominion, to subjugate)

(Genesis 2:5 and 8)

4. Adam was to _cultivate_ the ground ("abad" (Heb) – to till, dress it, to work as a servant)

5. Adam was to _keep_ the garden God had provided him. (protect life) ("shamar" (Heb) – to guard, to protect, to keep charge of – to treasure memories, to treasure memories, to observe, to watch over.

(Genesis 2:19-20)
6. Adam named all of the animals.

6. *(male and female)* **was given boundaries for his behaviors and curiosity.** (Genesis 2:15-17)

   1. Adam was provided food, and given instructions.

   2. Adam was protected from knowledge he was not ready for.

7. Adam needed an environment conducive for his design. (Genesis 2:7-15)

   1. This passage infers that God created the Garden in order to provide man with a sense of security and safety. It must have been a beautiful place. All of man's physical needs were met.

8. Adam needed community and relationship. (Genesis 2:18-25)

   1. It was <u>not good</u> for Adam to be alone; without a companion. This scripture infers that God created the animal kingdom for man's sense of belonging.

   2. In creating a companion for the man, God separated him into two parts; each with elements of the other. The souls became counterparts – mirror images in design -- that when put together, created a complete representation of their Creator.

      As male and female individuals, before the entrance of sin, the man and the woman each would have had an inner perception of the other's design. Relationship and communication would have held a main element of seeking to connect and remember that part now removed. Even though they were separate, and individual, they were not independent from one another. The bodies were separate, but their souls were able to unite and experience that same oneness with each other and with God they had had before the companion was formed.

   3. The man and woman not only had relationship and community with each other, as companions; they also had relationship and community with God – Father, Son and Holy Spirit. (Gen 1:26-28)

<u>**Clue Question #1**</u>

How does knowing God's original design for Adam: male & female affect your understanding of His design for you? How does it affect your understanding of your personal role in relationships?

Man/Woman's Design Prior to Sin

All elements of the Creation were in sync, and in unity with one another. Man and woman were created in the image of God. God is in total unity and agreement with Himself. Each element of His nature flows in and out of itself – He has perfect harmony. Each element affects the other.

Principle: Within Abba's design and creation, there is no separateness. Each part affects the whole.

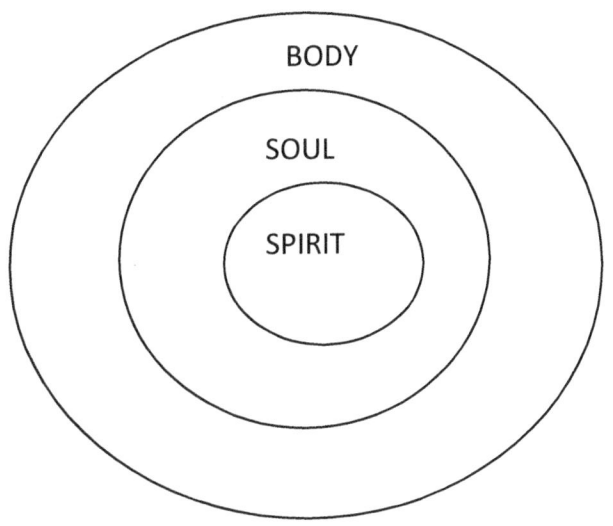

Unity is not sameness – or lack of uniqueness.

The Inner Flow of Man/Woman's Being Before the Fall

Before Sin entered the planet, man and woman were unaware; in a childlike state. They were innocent. Because they were unaware, they were naked, vulnerable, and had no reason to have secrets from each other. They could be easily known. They were completely trusting. They were full of motivation and excitement. Each day held expectation for Living.

Confident communion with God and each other
↓
Healthy Will (positive choices)
↓
God-ordered Mind/Peace
↓
Whole and vigorous Emotions/Contentment
↓
Truth-based Perceptions and Intuition
↓
Appetites were part of Unique Preferences
↓
Physical connection was part of the Need for Community

BEFORE SIN –

    There was no disease, or sickness. There were no broken trust issues. There was harmony in creation. There was no food chain. The weather patterns were in harmony – no destruction. There was no need for comfort. Every element **BELONGED.**

    There was no resistance or opposition; no blame, no rejection, no pain. There was no selfishness. There was no weakness, only strength.

    There was no disagreement or division. There was no abuse.

    Earth and the Heavenlies were in unity; harmonious with their Creator.

**ABBA FATHER WAS COMPLETELY IN CHARGE,
and had delegated SOME of His authority to the man and the woman**

The Sin-Damaged Design: Lost Paradise

What was lost?

1. Man and woman experienced death in their spiritual beings. Everyone born on the planet would now be born with a dead human spirit, waiting to be once again breathed upon by their Creator.

2. The ability to relate to God without fear was lost. Man and woman became aware of the difference between good and evil.

3. The Choice to Disobey/Disregard gave the man and woman's delegated rule of the planet to Satan. Man became a "son of disobedience."

What entered the planet?

1. Fear, Shame, Pride, Deception, Manipulation, Blame, Defensiveness, Hatred, Control, Denial, Blindness, Disease, Aggression, Resistance, Distortion, Sensuality, Confusion, Death, Decay, Negative emotions, Discontent, to name a few elements that were not present before Sin.

Expulsion from Eden –Gustave Dore

God still understood Adam; but Adam found he could not understand God. Moment by moment communication had ceased, although the connection was still longed for. Adam was now a sensual being. (Gen 3:8-11)

Adam now began a blind search to understand and embrace his design. He was still formed in the likeness of Creator, but now he did not have a goal or an imprinting available. (Genesis 1:27)

Adam, male and female, became two individuals who also could not reach the same connection they knew before Sin. Adam named his wife, "Eve." (Gen 3:20)

The Sense of Being CAST OUT, or CAST AWAY, is the main result of the Entrance of Sin… REJECTION and ABANDONMENT began to work accusation against God.

Man/Woman's Design Because of Sin

All elements of the Creation became out of sync, and became no longer in unity with one another. Although man and woman were created in the image of God, must be shown that connection. The concept of total unity is now foreign to man, because he is imprinted with sin and deception. However, God's nature is still the same, and the original design is still intact. Because of Sin, man is now divided and confused in his being. He cannot distinguish Truth from Error. There is no real harmony. However, each element still affects the other.

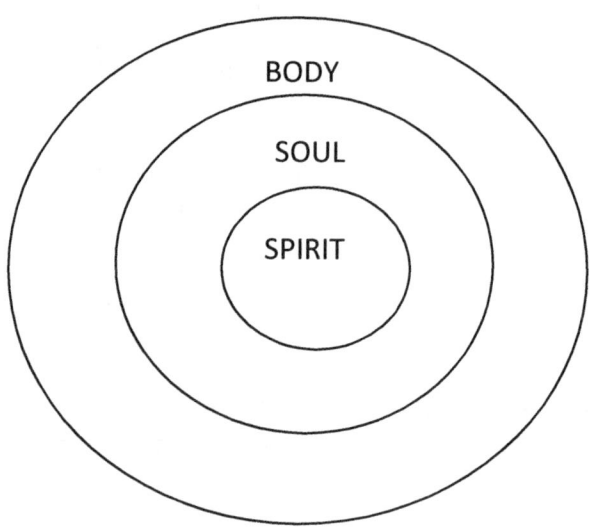

BECAUSE OF SIN –
    Man's physical body is prey to disease, and sickness.
    Man's soul has difficulty trusting. There is no harmony.
    The Food chain went into operation (God's limitation on Satan's destructiveness).
    Weather cycles, etc., began (God's limitation on Satan's destructiveness)
    Death and Destruction came to rule.
    Man's first need is now for comfort, and a sense of belonging.
    Resistance and opposition to God's rule began, along with Blame, Fear,
    Rejection, Pain, Shame, and Death. Self became the center of the human orbit.
    Weakness began to determine behavior, rather than God's Plan and purpose.
    Disagreement, division and abuse began.
    Earth and the Heavenlies became separated; with a great gulf between the
    physical and the spiritual realms, even though they still both exist simultaneously.

ABBA FATHER IS STILL COMPLETELY IN CHARGE.
However, because Adam (male and female) chose to become disobedient,
Adam's descendants must now choose. Abba Father will only
only rule in the physical realm where Satan's usurped rule is resisted and removed;
this happens through man's choice to once again become a "son of obedience."

The Inner Flow of Man/Woman's Being After the Fall

After Sin entered the planet, man and woman became aware; they were still in a childlike state, but now had no tooling for living life without God. No longer innocent, they became aware and prey to their appetites; they began to be driven by their pain and need for comfort. Because a bad choice, made in a vulnerable and naked state, had opened them to Pain, they began to cover themselves. They began to with-hold relationship, keep secrets, and put their trust in the wrong things. No longer easily known, they had to learn to communicate, but found themselves hampered by a lack of understanding and connection. Motivation and excitement died, unless personal gain was involved. Expectations for Living became tied to personal comfort and gratification.

Because of the choice to sin (disobey God) –
Man's self nature is now predisposed to choose disobedience, and self-gratification

> *Man sinned with his choices (his will – so his battle to do the right thing will be fought within his will.*
>
> *Woman sinned with her emotions; being deceived – so her battle to do the right thing will be fought within her thoughts and feelings.*

Desire for Self-Satisfaction/Gratification

Prioritized Physical Comfort/sensual
↓
Comfort based physical Appetites
↓
Self-centered Perceptions
↓
Self-centered emotions/discontent
↓
Confused/Embattled Mind
↓
Passive/Bruised human will
↓
Insecure intuitions/no communion
↓
Broken human spirit
↓
Seeking Comfort/Community

Jesus' Provision: Paradise Regained (The Kingdom of Heaven)

Genesis 3:6-7 and Genesis 3:21

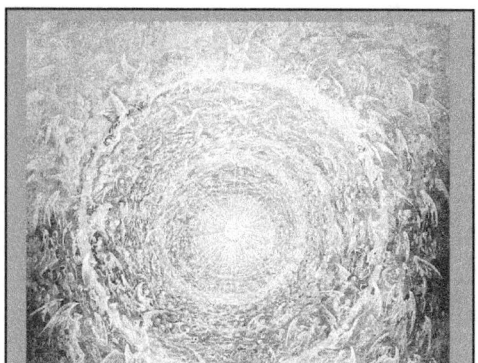

Rosa Celeste –Gustave Dore

It is God's Desire that we understand Him, and accept and know that He understands us. He wants us to have moment by moment communication between us. He wants us to experience spiritual life. (John 3:16; Psalm 103)

It is God's Desire that we understand and embrace who He has created us to be. We have been formed in the likeness of our Creator. (Philippians 1:6)

It is God's Desire that we experience and know Community and our part in His Design. (Ephesians 2:10) (Titus 2:13-14)

Clue Question #2

What do you understand about God's desire to relate to you on a deep and personal level, based on these scriptures and this information?

Notes:

The MakeUp of Man
II Corinthians 1:10 and I Thessalonians 5:23

1. **Body – The Vessel.** That part of man, which is physically seen and has tangible feeling. It's nature is understood by the abilities to touch, see, hear, smell and taste. It is the vehicle through which the desires and choices of the soul and spirit are expressed and carried out. (See Luke 12:22)

2. **Soul – The Sensual Portion.** That unseen part of man, which is the seat of his personality and desires. It's nature can be seen in man's ability to sense sentiment, whether painful or pleasurable (the emotions). The soul is also seen in the ability to choose, distinguishing between right and wrong. Choices in this area of man are made based upon those distinguishments. (the will). The soul also carries man's ability to think in reasonable patterns for development of communication and understanding (the mind). (See Matthew 22:37)

Prior to regeneration, the soul is under the bondage and dominion of Satan. It's natural nature is to be consumed with itself, and its own gratification. The soul must be made new and transformed into the likeness of Jesus following the re-birth of the spirit of man. (II Corinthians 3:18) The soul is the place of battle in the believer. **The soul is the unseen part of our being that is aware and drawn to the physical realm by its appetites. Before regeneration, it is unaware of the eternal realm.**

3. **Spirit -- The Eternal Connection.** That unseen part of man, which comprises his ability to communicate from the depths of his being with his Creator. It comprises his conscience, his inner spiritual sense, and his intuition. (John 3:1-20) Without regeneration by the Spirit of God, the spirit of man is dead and is full of the desire to sin. [Adam was made a living soul, and willfully gave the life of his spirit over to the enemy. Jesus Christ was made a quickening (life-giving, resurrecting) Spirit, so that all who call upon Him are able to be delivered – from darkness (the desire to sin, blindness) into light (the desire to please the Father). That choice to follow Christ and receive His gift of Life, brings a regeneration of the human spirit in the Inner man]. Regeneration is the only hope man has to regain the Pathway to eternal life and freedom lost by Adam's willful sin. (I Corinthians 15:44-45, Romans 6:5-11, John 3;16, Romans 5:8-19, and Romans 6:6) **The spirit is the unseen part of our being that is aware and drawn to the eternal realm through relationship with Jesus Christ and Abba Father.**

The Body --   affects our appetites, and our practical habit patterns

The human body is the portion of our being where the evidence of our personal choices and patterns shows itself.

    Proverbs 17:22   The attitude of the soul affects the health of the body.

    III John 2   The level of health in the soul, can be evidence by the physical level of health.

    Proverbs 18:14   Attitude is attached to infirmity (weakness in body/soul)

    Psalm 103:1-5   Worship and recognition of God's role in our lives is directly tied to our physical health.

Notes:

The Human spirit   affects our life approach attitudes

The human spirit affects our attitudes and our approach to living. When Sin has affected us in our human spirit, we can show various attitudes in our perceptions, as well as how we filter life experiences.

Isaiah 19:14	having an "errant" or "perverse" (distorted) spirit
Job 32:18	a "hasty" spirit
I Kings 21:5	a "sullen" spirit
Numbers 5:14	a "jealous" spirit
Psalm 15	a "broken" spirit

When we are born again, these life approach attitudes begin to be confronted by the Spirit of God, and we learn to choose Him instead of ourselves.

Our life approach attitudes determine our choices and our actions. This affects every area of our lives.

Notes:

The Soul   affects our choices, our thoughts, and our feelings

The human soul affects our patterns in daily living.

Romans 12:1-2	The <u>mind</u> must be renewed to think clearly, and according to God's patterns.
Luke 4:18 Psalm 139:23,24	The <u>emotions</u> must be healed to sense the Grace and presence of God; as he originally intended.
Joshua 24:5 Matthew 26:39/Luke 22:41-44 Hebrews 12:1-4	The <u>will</u> must be healed and strengthened to choose God's pathway. The battle to choose well and hold to those choices is the basis for personal identity formation.

The soul is the area of our lives where we choose what we believe, and what perceptions we will hold to. It is the area where we repress and suppress emotions. It is the area where we store trauma. It is the portion of our being that responds to stresses and to abuses. The is the place of battle.

Notes:

The Process of Regeneration and Growth

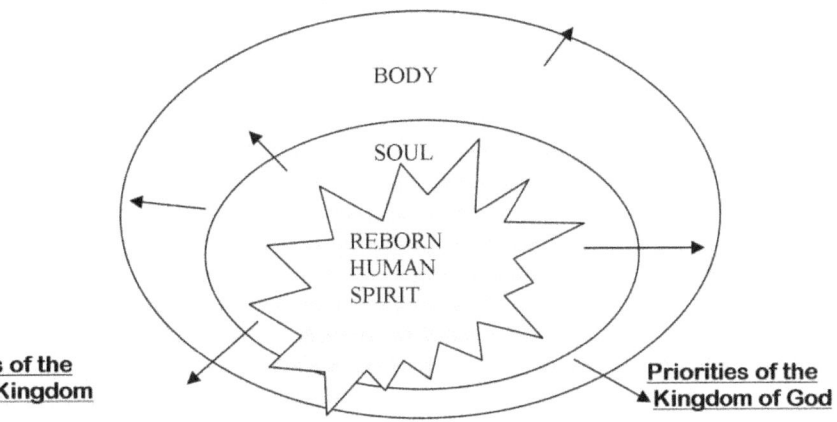

Priorities of the World's Kingdom

Priorities of the Kingdom of God

Motivation: *Making room for oneself*	**Motivation:** *Trusting Abba to make a way*
Driven by: Approval/Acceptance of Others / Fear of Rejection	**Led by:** Approval/Acceptance of Abba Father/Holy Spirit
Desire for Self-Satisfaction/Gratification	**The Ministry of the Holy Spirit**
Prioritized Physical Comfort/sensual	Physical comfort/stewardship
Comfort based physical Appetites	Disciplined appetites
Self-centered Perceptions	Truth based perceptions
Self-centered emotions/discontent	Consecrated Emotions/Content
Confused/Embattled Mind	Renewed Mind/Peace
Passive/Bruised human will	Intentional Will (positive choices)
Insecure intuitions/no communion	Confident communion
Broken human spirit	Submitted to change human spirit
Seeking Comfort/Community	Receiving the Ministry of the Holy Spirit
Principle: Without Christ, we seek comfort for our inner brokenness, and cater to ourselves in actions and attitude.	**Principle:** In Christ, we receive comfort and healing, carrying the Comforter within ourselves. Our first thought is no longer ourselves, but obedience, and relationship.

Trickle-Down Effect of the Fall

Psalm 1 "Planted Tree" Effect of Redemption

© 2007 atg

When we Come to God...

1. The original human creation was made in the image and likeness of our Creator. We are three-part, just as God is three-part.

2. Before sin, the human creation was spiritually alive; functioning in awareness of the spiritual realm; in constant connection and flow with the Creator. The visible and invisible were inter-connected. There was no separation between the realms.

3. After sin, separation occurred between the two realms. (Luke 16:26)
This invoked separation in all of the physical realm.
Unity was replaced with hierarchy.
Pride, Fear, Control replaced Love in the earthly realm.

Clue Question #3 –

In what areas of your life do you currently sense difficulty in relationships? What parts of you are involved with that difficulty? What would you like to see change in your ability to relate to others?

Points to Ponder

A. When we come to Jesus Christ, making Him the center of our life-orbit, His life envelopes our own.

    Colossians 3:2-4

B. His Grace covers our failings and mistakes.

    Ephesians 2:1-13

    Psalm 103:10-14

C. When He assesses our lives, He sees us as we will be and should be, not punishing us for our present condition.

    Ephesians 2:14-18

    re: enmity see Gen. 3:15

D. His Blood has become the filter through which our lives are to be seen – not only by Him, but by ourselves and by other people.

    Hebrews 12:18-24

Notes:

Residual effects of Sin and the Entrance of Sin Nature

Dona Mar – Pablo Picasso

1. Distortion of the Image of God

2. Shattering of the Human Personality

3. The spirit of the world rules the atmosphere of the planet (I Cor. 2:12/James 4:4)

4. The flesh (sin nature in man's soul) seeks to influence our choices (Galatians 5:13-26)

5. The devil seeks to destroy, derail, devour, and discourage us, bringing us under his influence and dominion. (Ephesians 6:11-12/I Peter 5:8)

6. The accusation and blame mechanisms against God, ourselves and others began to voice themselves, as expressions of Sin's rule.

7. Fragmentation of Soul, and the Ability to Relate/Connect

Relational Principle #1 –

Human beings are inherently self-centered, without ability or capacity to give or receive love outside of relationship with God, because **God is love**. Jesus Christ is God.

Grace – *"The beauty and elegance of God's character, that has freely given His favor and blessing to us. He has given us immunity, good will, pardon, and abundant kindness. This is poured out on us without limit or condition, just because we have chosen to believe, accept, follow and identify with Him in how we approach and live our lives."*

The Doorway back to the Original Design – Jesus Christ

The Human Spirit – When we are in Jesus, this part of us is sealed and safe from destruction (unless we willfully choose to turn away from God.)

2 Corinthians 1:19-22 –

Ephesians 1:11-14

Ephesians 4:30

The Human Body – When we are in Jesus, this part of us is called "a vessel," or "a temple for God."

Romans 9:21

I Thessalonians 4:4

I Corinthians 3:16

I Corinthians 6:19

The Human Soul – When we are in Jesus, this part of us is under continual reconstruction, needing repentance (change), and development. This is the hard work of discipleship.

The soul is our mind, will and emotions (what we think, choose and feel).

Mind --*Romans 12:1-2-- The mind must be renewed to think clearly, and according to God's patterns.*

Emotions -- Luke 4:18/ Psalm 139:23,24 -- The emotions must be healed to sense the Grace and presence of God; as he originally intended.

Will -- Joshua 24:5/ Matthew 26:39/Luke 22:41-44/ Hebrews 12:1-4 -- The will must be healed and strengthened to choose God's pathway. The battle to choose well and hold to those choices is the basis for personal identity formation.

Philippians 2:5-16 –

Galatians 4:19 – ("formed" = *morpho*) *idea of forming, and then appearing.*
"metamorphoo" -- to be changed into another form –

II Corinthians 3:18

Romans 12:2

The Great Separation affected everything in Creation.

It invoked Distancing (the desire to be without help/counsel), and the desire for independence –

<u>From God</u>   Isaiah 59:1-2

                                                   Proverbs 19:3

<u>From all the attributes of God</u>
(Truth, Love, Community, Health)   Galatians 5:19-21

<u>From others</u>   Proverbs 18:1

                                                   I Corinthians 12:

<u>From ourselves</u>   Jeremiah 17:9

                                                   I Thessalonians 5:23

<u>Principle:</u>
God does not separate Himself from us ….
Our choices create the separation – We are the ones who have
continually removed ourselves from Him, and His influence.

<u>What that means when it comes to our ability to live and grow –</u>
The ability to have consistent, congruent, life-flow has been damaged, stopped, and/or hindered. Then, in that place, it is Sin's nature to accuse Father God of rejecting us.

Bonded-ness begins with God -
The first step is the un-working of Separation from His Nature.

What God actually has said —

Luke 12:32

Psalm 27:10

Isaiah 40:11

Jeremiah 31:3

Psalm 84:11

Lamentations 3:22

Hebrews 13:8

Clue Question #4—
How have the elements of abandonment, independence, loneliness and isolation affected your understanding and image of God? How does what we have learned in this class change/confront what you have thought to be true before now?

This Week:

*1. **Journal** your answers to the four questions presented in the class materials. Use a separate journal notebook to log your answers if needed. Please think through your answers. It will help you later in the class to consider why you have answered each question the way you have.... As we walk through the class sessions, the answers you present to the Clue Questions will help you a great deal in understanding what steps to take for your personal growth and development, even after the classes have ended.*

*2. **Read** chapters 1, 2 and 3 of "The Family" by John Bradshaw. Make notes on the questions that rise as you read. Also write out discoveries you make from the reading, and connections you make to the class teaching materials.*

*3. At some point during the week, before the next class session, please try to take time to **Study/Re-read** the Scriptures listed regarding the attitude of God towards us as His creation. Choosing to believe – really believe – what He has said about you is extremely important in learning to take the next step in discovering the Secrets for Relational Living.*

Session Two — "What is a Bonded Person?"

What we will learn in this Session:

We were created as God's children for the purpose of relationship and growth. Part of our discipleship as believers in Jesus Christ is the call to become mature in Him. There is no short-cut to this, or quick-fix for our difficulties. We will study the levels of Moral and Cognitive Development, and how those levels address where we are personally living. The student will learn the purpose of healthy bonding, and the description of a well-bonded individual.

The Instructor's Goal for this Session:

To help the student discover personal levels of mis-addressed or un-addressed bonding, beginning the personal connection process with present patterns of living, with a healthy alternate goal in mind.

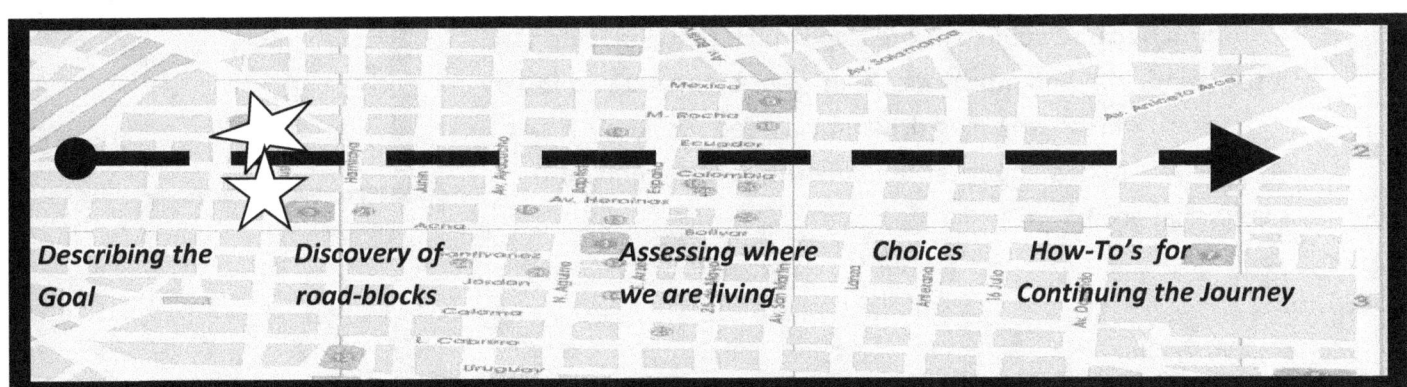

Describing the Goal — Discovery of road-blocks — Assessing where we are living — Choices — How-To's for Continuing the Journey

Session Two—What is a bonded person?

Let's Review

1. God's original design of creation was filled with connected-ness, bonded-ness, and relationship. Adam, male and female were connected with God; they were connected with each other; within their own beings there was personal understanding and confidence of their unique design. Adam, male and female had been formed in the likeness of his Creator, and had an automatic desire to copy the model and imprinting He provided them. (Genesis 1:27)

2. Within relationship, there was unity. Unity is not same-ness. Just as in God's nature there is distinctive uniqueness, man and woman were designed to be the same way, with each one in connection and unity with each other.

3. After sin entered the planet, everything changed. The original design and plan of God for relationship became unattainable outside of relationship with God. The spiritual part of man died, and could no longer understand or relate to God, who is Spirit.

4. Rather than being a primarily spiritual being, man and woman became soulish in their approach to living; ruled by the mind, will and emotions. Man went being led and fed by the Spirit of God, to being driven by a need for comfort and approval. Man's appetites became the center of his or her personal orbit.

5. The planet itself became subject to the rule of Satan, the usurper. Whereas before sin, all of creation had been filled with the glory and Presence of God, and in relationship with Him; after sin, creation experienced what it meant to be outside of the glory and Presence of God.
To protect all of us from having to remain in this state forever, God prevented Adam and Eve from also taking from the Tree of Life (eternal life), sending them from the Garden of Eden.

The Sense of Being CAST OUT, or CAST AWAY, is the main result of the Entrance of Sin... REJECTION and ABANDONMENT began to work accusation against God.

6. This sense of "outside" is the basis of all separation issues that we as humans experience in our lives and relationships on planet earth.

Notes:

Jesus Christ is God, come in the form of His Creation, to show us the way back into relationship with the Father. He is the BRIDGE.

Contrasting Kingdoms

Original Design	Satan's Realm	God's Kingdom Now
Innocence	Cynicism	Belief (Forgiveness)
Love	Fear	Love
Trust	Broken Trust	Trust
Unity/Flow	Independence	Unity/Flow
Confident relationship	Intimidation/Domination	Team/Family Dynamic
No division	Self-gratification	Mutual Respect/Body-life

Within us:	Galatians 5:19-21	Galatians 5:22-24
Body, soul and spirit were in flow, content, and in harmony with God	Our natural desire is to believe that we are separated from God by God's design – rejected. Many times, we only are aware of negative emotions.	We are called to choose to believe God, above what our natural desire for comfort, and appetites dictate.
Man's spirit ruled him, led by the Spirit of God.	Man's soul (mind, will and emotions) rules him, and seeks his own comfort and gratification first.	Man is designed to strengthen his re-born spirit, and through a growth process, experience the healing and growth of his soul to adulthood.

> ***Note: If there had never been a separation, there would be no need for bonding. Separate-ness creates the need to bond, or attach.***

Clue Question #5-(2)

Looking at the middle column in the three columns above (page 26), circle the areas you find yourself battling when it comes to maintaining relationships in your life.

Considering what you have circled, what is the solution (or goal) that relates to it from the third column above? Write those solutions here (or on the journaling pages at the end of this book.)

II Peter 3:18   *auxanō—to increase, grow up*

Ephesians 4:12-16   *auxanō—to increase, grow up*

                                                           hēlikia—to mature to adulthood

---

I Corinthians 13:11-12   (became) *ginomai—come into being*

                                                           (man) *anēr—adult*

                                                           (childish) *nēpios - infant; untaught, unskilled*

In light of these Scriptures, what does it mean to "grow up?"

Relational Principle #2 –

Spiritual development and emotional maturity are intricately connected and cannot be separated.

Growth in these areas of life happens inter-dependently.

Clue Question #6-(2)

On the following scale, rate the level of experiential distance you experience in your relationship with God. (circle a number)

0	1	2	3	4	5	6	7	8	9	10	11	12
I don't feel God at all. Why try?			I have sensed His Presence at times past I wish I could now.				I sometimes experience His Presence, but it is work for me.					I can focus on Him and experience Him.

(The experiencing of an inner sense of relationship with God, is directly related to our emotional development, and our ability to bond/reciprocate in relationships.)

Levels and Stages of Personal Development

IQ	IQ—cognitive/ability to grasp facts (Piaget)	EQ	EQ – moral and emotional/ ability to relate (Kohlberg)	Notes:
Birth to age 2	1. <u>Sensorimotor</u> – We learn motor skills and reflexes from movement. We learn we are individuals in an environment. We respond to those in our circle. We cannot care for ourselves.	**Level 1** **Pre-conventional Morality**	**Stage 1 - Obedience & Punishment** We see rules as fixed and absolute. Obeying the rules helps us to avoid punishment. **Stage 2 - Individualism & Exchange** We see the best course of action as being the one that best serves our own individual needs. Reciprocity is possible, but only if it serves our own interest. ("Me" first).	
Age 3-7 – when speech skills begin	2. <u>Pre-operational</u> – We learn to use symbols to represent objects. We personalize objects. We can grasp and remember events not at hand. We gradually learn to conceptualize time. We are deeply influenced by fantasy—how we wish things would be. We assume everyone shares our perceptions and viewpoint. We change information to fit our own ideas.	**Level 2** **Conventional Morality**	**Stage 3 - Interpersonal Relationships** We see ourselves as "good" or "bad" focusing on living up to social expectations and roles. Conformity is emphasized, as is "being nice". We learn how our choices influence relationships.	
Age 7/8-12 low reading level to early adolescence	3. <u>Concrete</u> – We develop the ability to think abstractly and make rational judgments. We can observe and relate to situations. We can accept facts without changing them. We begin to ask questions to understand.	**Level 2** **Conventional Morality** (Cont'd)	**Stage 4 - Maintaining Social Order** We see ourselves as part of a greater group within society when making judgments. We learn to maintain safety and order by following rules and doing the right thing (our duty). We respect authority.	
Age 12+	4. <u>Formal</u> – We become able to make rational judgments without concrete objects. We become capable of hypothetical and deductive reasoning. We can see more than one perspective in order to learn and grow.	**Level 3 –** **Post-Conventional Morality**	**Stage 5 - Social Contract & Individual Rights** We begin to account for differing values, opinions and beliefs in others. We see our need to agree upon laws & standards with the consideration of others. **Stage 6 - Universal Principles** We possess internalized principles of justice and moral reasoning. We learn to follow these internalized principles even if they conflict with external rules and laws.	

Clue Question #7-(2)

Looking at the last page (page 32), list here, the level you can honestly say you are living in regard to the IQ stages (Left side).

What physical age correlates to that stage of cognitive development?

Looking at the last page (page 32), list here the level you can honestly say you are living in regard to the EQ stages (right side). – what stage?

In considering the EQ levels of development, where do you believe the majority of human society lives in day to day practice? (what stage?)

How, do you think, has living on that level affected the depth of believers in their personal discipleship in the Body of Christ as a whole?

Levels of Attachment and Conscience Development

Unbonded Unattached	Fragile Or untooled in Bonding	Incomplete Or fractional Bonding	Damaged Or weakened Attachment	Standard or Normal Bonding	Well-Bonded and Attached
Serial Killers Sexual Violence (for pleasure)	Criminals Thieves Prostitutes	Thrill-seekers Some Spies "Danger" addicts	"Charmers," slick presenters, some politicians, "The show must continue mindset"	Intact & well-adjusted families/healthy relaitonships	Humanitarians Those who give their lives for others
Sociopaths Psycopaths (Ted Bundy) (Charles Mansen) (Adolph Hitler)			Narcissists (ego-driven) Prima Donnas		Philanthropists Missionaries (Teresa of Calcutta) (Albert Schweitzer)

FEAR Driven → LOVE Led

Unattached; Unbonded / Dulled; Evil Conscience

- Un-motivated
- Taker from others
- Wrong moral choices
- Critical, laughs at other's pain
- Manipulation, "con"
- Rejects relationship
- Feels nothing
- Stubborn, has no need
- Silent, stoic
- Refuses Truth, alternates own view
- Negative flow
- No hope or future
- Violence
- Closed, impassive
- Bloody images, death

Attachment Disorders / Impaired Conscience

- motivated by gain
- non-contributor
- passive
- laughs at others
- dishonesty, charmer
- hiding in group, loner
- feels negative emotion
- argumentative, debating
- responds only
- argues with Truth
- sporadic flow
- half-empty perspective
- sarcasm, anger
- narcissist in heart, abusive
- abnormal fears, depressed

Healthy Attachment / Healthy Conscience

- self-disciplines evident
- giving to others
- solid moral choices
- sense of humor, laughs at self
- honesty
- ability to relate
- ability to feel and process emotion
- teachable
- has an ability to communicate
- Understands and applies Truth
- creative flow
- half-full perspective
- gentleness
- openness of heart
- normal fears

Notes:

Clue Question #8-(2)

Looking at the last page (page 34), read the columns describing the various descriptions of relational living in regard to attachments and conscience development. Then, make a mark on each line to show where you currently live in your emotional development with other people. If you find you are between two of the descriptions, utilize the line as an incremental scale of progression.

The Qualities of a Bonded Person

1. **Self-disciplines evident** -- self starter, possesses inner motivations

2. **Giving to others** – equal sharing in relationship; not selfish

3. **Solid moral choices** – is able to hold to what is morally healthy, for self and the common good

4. **Sense of humor, can laugh at self** – can own personal mistakes without anger or blame

5. **Honesty** – speaks the Truth with self and others; applies Truth for change without complaint

6. **Ability to relate** – sees self as part of a larger whole; honors others' input; does not operate in status mindset

7. **Ability to feel emotion** – experiences joy and contentment; not driven or "shut-down"

8. **Teachable** -- realizes personal need to learn; non-defensive

9. **Ability to communicate** – offers perspective for consideration; listens to others; responding and sharing

10. **Understanding Truth** – accepts absolutes; does not substitute protection mechanisms (or intentions) for actions

11. **Creative Flow** -- perceives direction; contributes for the greater good; shares ideas

12. **Half full perspective** – moves in an attitude of thankfulness and sees the whole picture, not just personal sphere

13. **Gentleness** – without defensiveness; processes pain to understand purpose; is kind

14. Openness of heart — *is easily known; understands and practices healthy boundaries, sees others' pain as well as own*

15. Normal fears -- *is wise in decision-making and direction, expects to succeed, sees failure as opportunity for growth*

Note: All of the elements present in healthy relationships, as well as the ability to bond, are completely absent in natural living – that is, outside of the nature of God.

Clue Question #9-(2)

What connections have you discovered this week in regard to the need for emotional development and bonding? Make a note of those discoveries here.

This Week:

1. __Journal__ your answers to the five questions presented in the class materials. You can answer the questions in this book, or in another journal. Please think through your answers. The Clue Questions are designed to help you make discoveries as we walk through the class, and help you chart your own discipleship path in these areas of living.

2. __Read__ chapters 4, 5 and 6 of "The Family" by John Bradshaw. Make notes on the questions that rise as you read. Also write out discoveries you make from the reading, and connections you make to the class teaching materials.

3. At some point during the week, before the next class session, please try to take time to __Study/Re-read__ scriptural exhortations provided in this session's notes, as well as the outlines on the levels of development from pages 32 and 34. As you do so, contemplate regarding your life-steps in regard to this class. Where would you like your spiritual and emotional development to be? Prayerfully set a personal goal for your growth – what would you like to understand? Where would you like to experience more maturity and development? Ask the Holy Spirit to speak to your heart about what your next step in personal growth will be. Taking these steps before session 3 will help you to be ready for the next step in discovering the Secrets for Relational Living.

Session Three — "Levels of Development"

What we will learn in this Session:

We will learn what it means to have a personal relationship life-orbit. We will learn what mechanisms prevent relationship, and we will discover the differing depths of communication and relationship. We will also introduce the concept of human bonding needs, and the necessary approval messages each of us must receive for a healthy childhood experience. We will also discover the how the filters of Fear and Pride affect our ability to give and receive love. This will be tied to Jesus' first parable, "The Sower and the Seed."

A personal discovery worksheet is provided after this class session, to enable the student to make application of the information disclosed to this point in the class.

The Instructor's Goal for this Session:

To help the student make further discovery of personal levels of mis-addressed or un-addressed bonding, continuing the personal connection process with present patterns of living, with a healthy alternate goal in mind.

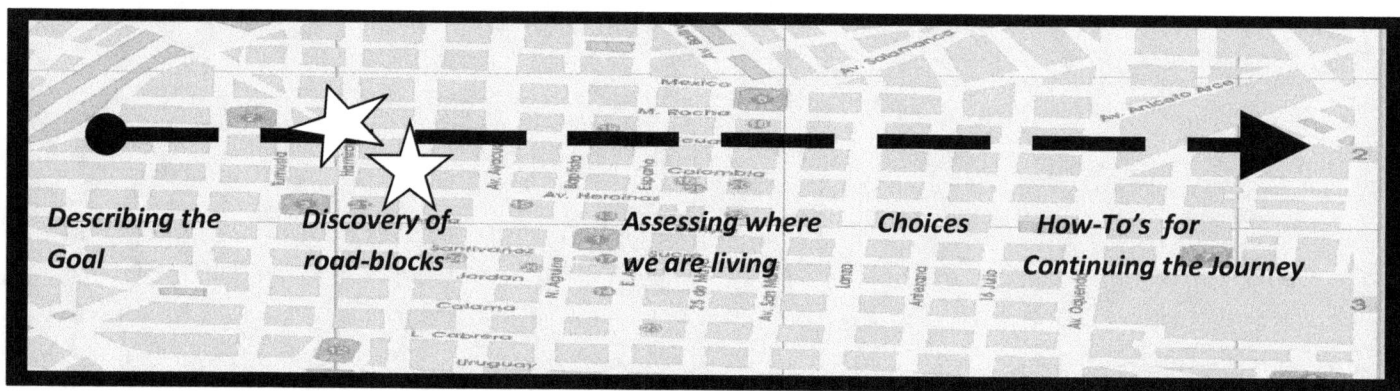

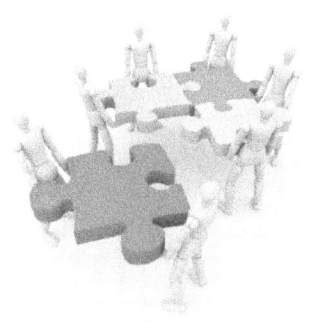

Session Three—
"Levels of Development"

Let's Review

Relational Principle #1 –
Human beings are inherently self-centered, without ability or capacity to give or receive love outside of relationship with God, because <u>God is love</u>. Jesus Christ is God.

Relational Principle #2 –
Spiritual development and emotional maturity are intricately connected and cannot be separated. Growth in these areas of life happens inter-dependently.

God is Love (emotional maturity) --   *(I John 3:1-3 and 16-20)* --
                                                 (I John 4:15-20)

God is Spirit (spiritual development)   *(John 4:23-24)*

How needed are both of these elements of God's nature in your own life?
Is it possible to have either of these elements in our lives without God and be healthy?

> *In our growth/journey to become mature in our personal discipleship, we will experience battle within the soul (mind, will and emotions) between these three personal life-orbit patterns.*

1

<u>Motivated by Self-Approval</u>. A self-centered orbit is the natural (untouched by God) order. It is the basis of narcissism, and a closed orbit. *(Closed)*

2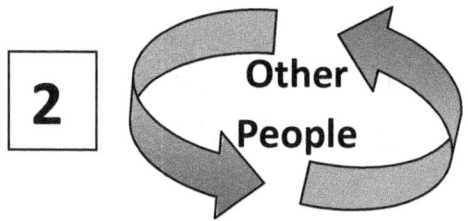

<u>Motivated by Man's Approval</u>. A people-centered orbit is the natural (untouched by God) imitation of God's order. It is the basis of inverted narcissism, or co-dependency. *(Partially closed)*

3

<u>Motivated by God's Approval</u>. A God-centered orbit is the super-natural (touched by God) order of the Spirit-formed believer. It is the life of the intentional disciple then the bond-servant. *(Open)*

<u>Clue Question #10-(3)</u>
In looking at the above three orbits, take a few moments to consider areas of your life where you find yourself battling in your ability to live relationally. Which one seems to give you the most difficulty in the midst of the process? Make a note here.

The Qualities of a Bonded Person

1. **Self-disciplines evident** -- *self starter, possesses inner motivations*

2. **Giving to others** – *equal sharing in relationship; not selfish*

3. **Solid moral choices** – *is able to hold to what is morally healthy, for self and the common good*

4. **Sense of humor, laugh at self** – *can own personal mistakes without anger or blame*

5. **Honesty** – *speaks the Truth with self and others; applies Truth for change without complaint*

6. **Ability to relate** – *sees self as part of a larger whole; honors others' input; does not operate in status mindset*

7. **Ability to feel emotion** – *experiences joy and contentment; not driven or "shut-down"*

8. **Teachable** -- *realizes personal need to learn; non-defensive*

9. **Ability to communicate** – *offers perspective for consideration; listens to others; responding and sharing*

10. **Understanding Truth** – *accepts absolutes; does not substitute protection mechanisms (or intentions) for actions*

11. **Creative Flow** -- *perceives direction; contributes for the greater good; shares ideas*

12. **Half full perspective** – *moves in an attitude of thankfulness and sees the whole picture, not just personal sphere*

13. **Gentleness** – *without defensiveness; processes pain to understand purpose; is kind*

14. Openness of heart — *is easily known; understands and practices healthy boundaries, sees others' pain as well as own*

15. Normal fears -- *is wise in decision-making and direction, expects to succeed, sees failure as opportunity for growth*

> *Note: All of the elements present in healthy relationships, as well as the ability to bond, are completely absent in natural living – that is, outside of the nature of God.*

Notes:

<u>**Clue Question #11-(3)**</u>

Looking at the Qualities of A Bonded Person list on pages 42-43, list here the qualities you find difficult to emulate or practice in relationships in your life.

Does the difficulty present itself with close relationships, working relationships, or with strangers? Make a note of that here.

"Secrets for Relational Living"

Giving & Receiving Love - Filters and Motivations

Receives the Love of God & applies it to own heart	Motivated and Influenced by Fear	Motivated and Influenced by Pride
1. Operates in discernment	1. Operates in suspicion	1. Operates in assumptions
2. Is a disciple - asks questions	2. Follows without question	2. Makes statements: already "understands"
3. Trusts with an open heart	3. Is afraid to trust: creates situations to avoid change	3. Moves independently: sees no need to trust
4. Seeks community: sees a need to grow	4. Anticipates repetition of prior wounds	4. Admits no vulnerability
5. Is teachable - without arguments	5. Desires to be taught, but thinks growth is Unattainable	5. Always has answers: Must "know" and be seen as having it all together
6. Seeks to change self	6. Wants other people to change them – is afraid to take steps on their own – is afraid to fail	6. Seeks to change others, while applying no change personally
7. Is willing to wait patiently	7. Gives up when no results are seen quickly - assumes failure	7. Manipulates circumstances for desired outcome
8. Has no agenda	8. Must have control of own environment	8. Must have personal rights acknowledged
9. Responds kindly	9. Guarded responses/silence	9. Unfeeling responses: factual
10. Accepts responsibility for own mistakes	10. Blames self	10. Blames others
11. Receives love unconditionally	11. Must reciprocate to keep a balance – fears rejection. Argues with love and forgiveness of God.	11. Sets criteria in order to be loved – sets terms and conditions. Actions not on the personal "list" are not seen as love. Argues with the love of God. Must earn significance.
12. Gives love unconditionally	12. Loves in order to find acceptance. Expressed gratitude/apologies are deemed as undeserved.	12. Loves in order to gain control. Expressed gratitude/apologies are deemed as not good enough.
13. Operates relationally	13. Anticipates rejection	13. Operates alone. Has no real need for others.
14. Keeps no record of wrongs	14. Keeps a list of personal wounds, to confirm and reinforce stalled growth	14. Keeps a list of others' failings – in order to maintain a sense of superior standing - holds others "accountable". Makes demands.
I Cor. 13/Psalm 103 – Sees God as a Loving Father. Growing in stature and nature of Christ.	John 5:1-9/II Tim 1:7 - Sees God as a chess Player. Is crippled in heart and feels inwardly broken. Is waiting for "Perfect Moment and Perfect Time." Lives intimidated Struggles with depression.	James 4:1-10/II Peter 2:11-25 - Sees God as The Ultimate Control, overpowering. Is blind and deaf, trying to "find" his own way. Battles with anger and frustration.

"Secrets for Relational Living"

The Journey Into Inner Life

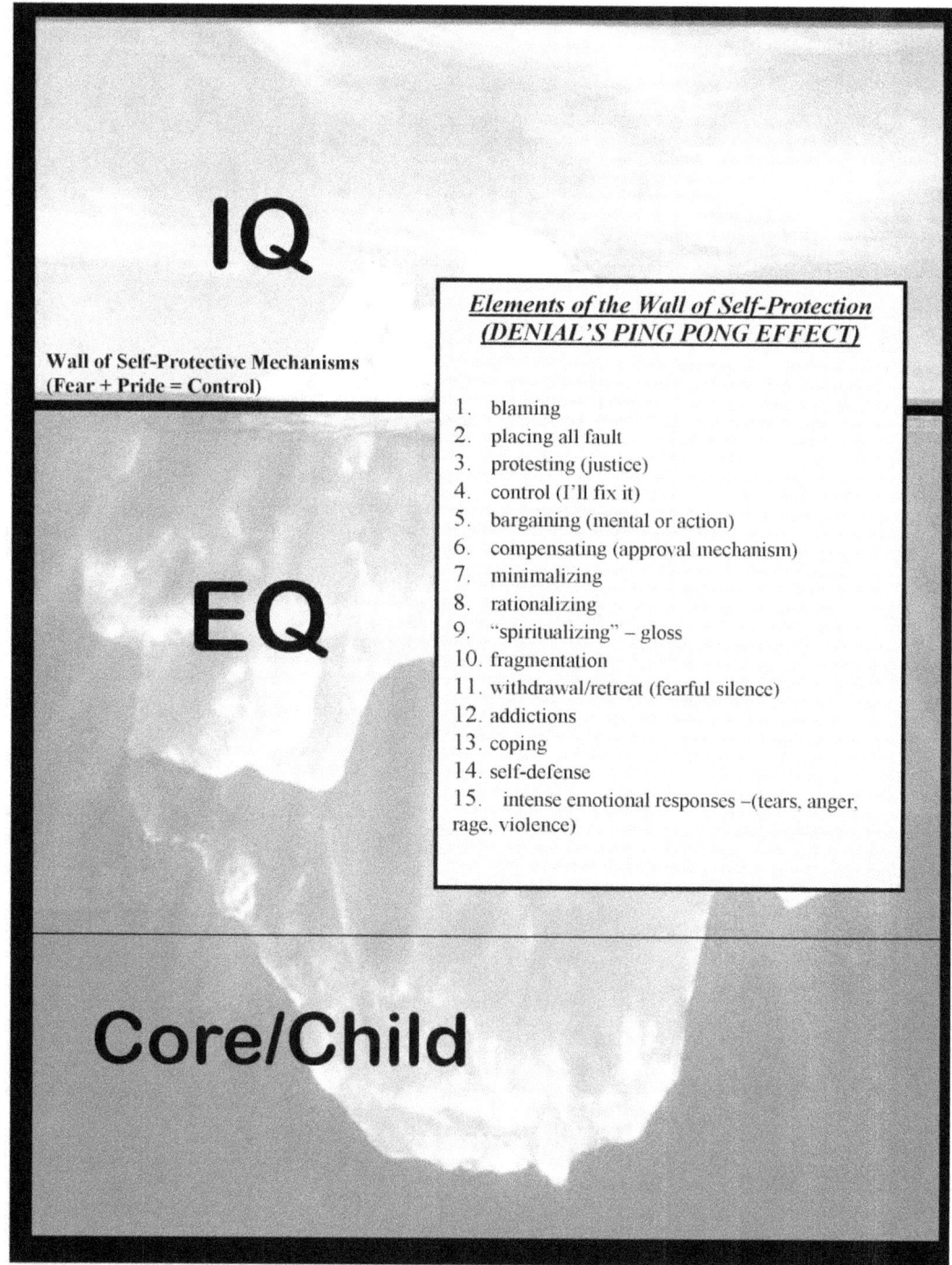

IQ

Wall of Self-Protective Mechanisms
(Fear + Pride = Control)

EQ

Core/Child

Elements of the Wall of Self-Protection
(DENIAL'S PING PONG EFFECT)

1. blaming
2. placing all fault
3. protesting (justice)
4. control (I'll fix it)
5. bargaining (mental or action)
6. compensating (approval mechanism)
7. minimalizing
8. rationalizing
9. "spiritualizing" – gloss
10. fragmentation
11. withdrawal/retreat (fearful silence)
12. addictions
13. coping
14. self-defense
15. intense emotional responses –(tears, anger, rage, violence)

Levels of Communication

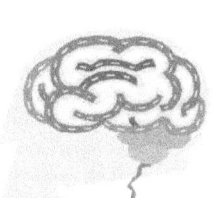

1. Clichés   Task & Doing

2. Facts

IQ   **IMAGE BASED**

Outer Life

Tangible

Wall of self protection—pride+fear=control

Inner Life   Intangible

3. Principles/Values/Morals Feelings

4. Yearnings/Needs   Relationship & Being

EQ   **TRUTH BASED**

Line of selfless choice

IQ & EQ   5. Deep sense of security & approval/Child   **OBEDIENCE BASED**

© dg atg

"Secrets for Relational Living"

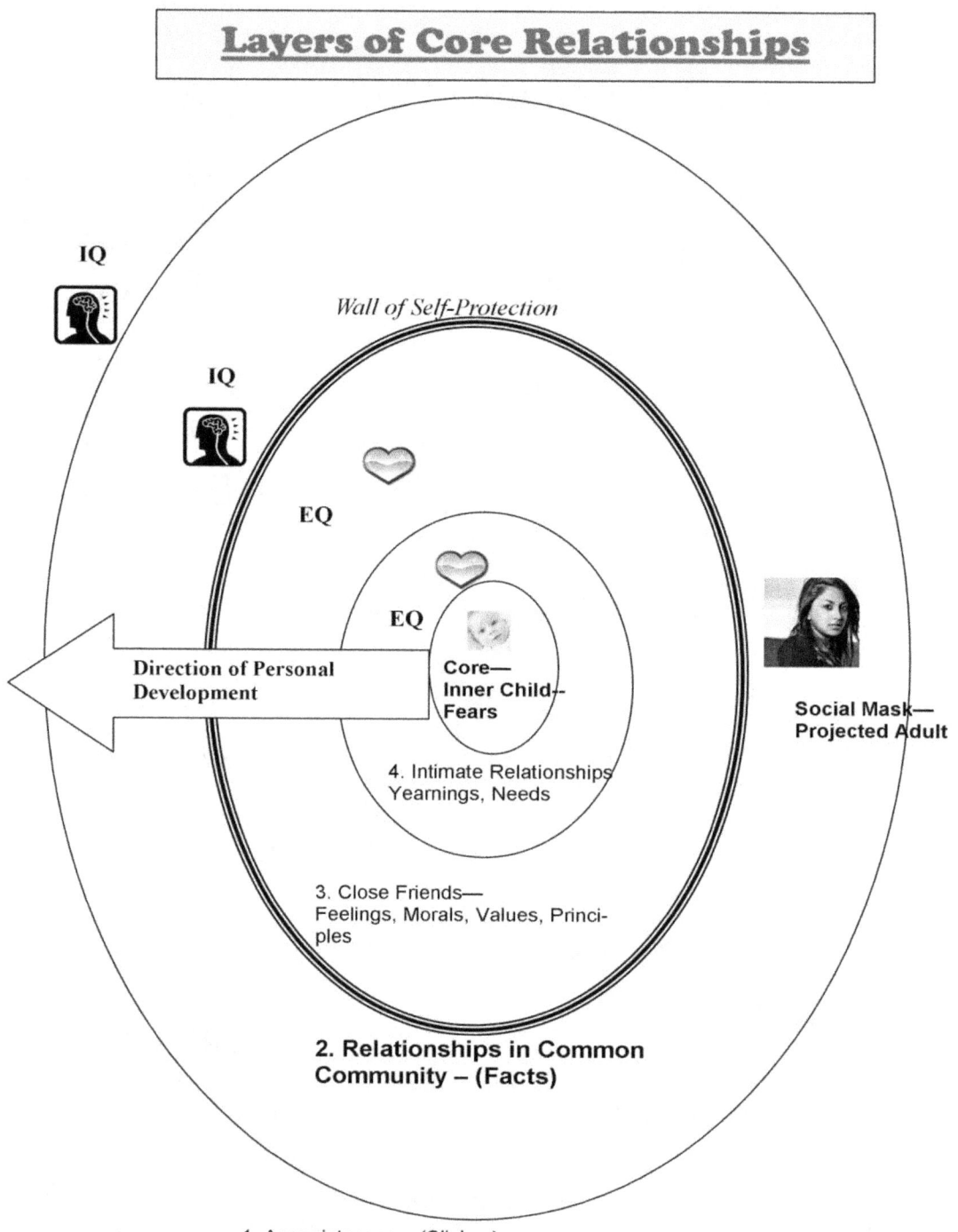

"Secrets for Relational Living"

Core Desires for Human Development

Principle: To reach a deeper level with health, the foundational needs of each prior level must have been addressed within the life. Without this, the person will continually sense a personal emptiness.

How Relationships form in Adult Life

Moral Development Levels Where life (interaction) Takes place	Core Need "To Know that I am able…"	Core Desire message received as approval
1. **IQ – Cliches**	To be "normal"	to be praised to be noticed
2. **IQ- Facts**	To "matter"	to be seen to be safe to be included to be affirmed	12+ yrs

~~~Self Protective Defense Mechanisms (Pride/Fear)~~~~~~~~~~~~~~~~~~~~

Gaps in bonding create inner

3. **EQ – values/principles** morals, feelings	To "be in the group"	to be touched(safe) to be heard to belong to be received	5-12 yrs
4. **EQ – yearnings/needs**	To be "at home in all settings"	to be safe/secure to be chosen to be understood to be included	18m-5yrs

~~~~~~~~~~~Line of Choice (Selflessness)~~~~~~~~~~~~~~~~~~~~~~~~~~

0-18mos

| 5. **IQ&EQ –**
Core Congruency
(Inner Child) | To have something unique to offer/ sense of belonging | to be safe
to be chosen
to be wanted/ chosen |

How Bonding influences development

- 48 -

"Secrets for Relational Living"

Clue Question #12-(3)

Take a look at the chart on page 45, "The Journey Into Inner Life." What self-protective mechanisms (from the list in the shaded box) have you seen modeled in relationships so far in your life? Which ones have your personally utilized? Make a list here.

Consider – How do these defense mechanisms keep you from connecting with those people in your life, with whom you would like a closer relationship? Write your observations here.

"Secrets for Relational Living"

Clue Question #13-(3)

Now, consider the chart on page 48, "Core Desires for Human Development." From the "core desire" column (message received as approval), make note of the emotional support you received in your formative years. In what ways were those desires met? Make a list here.

Now, looking at the same list, make note of the emotional support you realize was missing in your formative years. Make a list here.

> Relational Principle #3 –
> Our experiences, imprintings and relationships in early life development are catalysts for our deep perceptions and core beliefs regarding ourselves and how life works. Elements that have hindered healthy living are destructive and must be addressed, owned and healed.

Clue Question #14-(3)

Consider the statement in Relational Principle #3, above. What discoveries are you making regarding your ability to relate to others, and the reasons why you relate the way you do? Write those discoveries here.

The Sower and the Seed: Becoming A Cultivated & Well Watered Garden

"The Lord will guide you continually, and satisfy your soul in drought, and strengthen your bones, and you shall be like a watered garden, and like a spring of water, whose waters do not fail." Isaiah 58:11

The Parable: Matthew 13:3-9 and 18-23

Type of Soil Vs 3-9	Jesus' Meaning vs 18-23	Condition of the Heart	A Gardener's Solution	Spiritual Application
1. Seed on the wayside -- was devoured by birds	Not understood. Devil steals it. Survivor mentality	Numb, Trodden down. By reason of conditioning has become rock hard feels used.	Soak with water. Break up crusty earth. Dig deep earth. Dig. Remove rocks. Add fertilizer and conditioners before planting. Feed well.	Has learned to believe a lie. Life experiences have wounded and closed the heart. (emotionally and spiritually)
2. Seed on stony places -- no depth, withered by elements	Receives, but has no depth in himself to make application, is offended by difficulty and falls away only. No joy. "Tell me what the rules are – I'll do that."	Unaware of deeper possibilities. Too many hard things with no understanding or ability to resolve. Functioning plants well.	Water well to loosen earth. Remove stones. Dig down to rock. Add fertilizer and conditioners. Feed well.	Sees the stones. Feel stuck. Difficulties argue with the love of God. The heart wants to trust, but fears repetition of pain. (trusts self most)
3. Seed among thorns -- new growth crowded by weeds	Receives, but has so many other things "going on right now" any application is squeezed out, becomes unfruitful	Aware of deeper growth. Drawn by Holy Spirit -- is easily distracted by obligations and responsibilities. Content to maintain on surface but lives unfulfilled	Weed out crowded growth beds. Spade around plants for aerating soil. Add fertilizer. Condition soil. Water well. Monitor for sprouts of weed seeds not pulled on first try.	Is weed aware, assumes they are normal – is used to emotional clutter. Fearful of Change – task oriented for security. (works based. Condemnation focused, fear driven)
4. Seed on good ground -- yielded a crop	Receives, understands, allows it to grow, and bears life- fruit	Open and vulnerable. Teachable, receiving truth and making application personal changes daily indicate growth	Maintain weed free status. Maintain condition of soil. Regular cultivation and aeration for health. New plantings and pruning as applicable.	Maturity takes time, growth takes time. There are no substitutes. Discipleship involves discovery. Emotional health and spiritual maturity cannot be separated. Daily maintenance will ensure continued development.

This Week:

1. __Journal__ your answers to the five questions presented in the class materials, using either this book, or another journal. Please think through your answers. Then, considering your answers, and before the next session, complete Worksheet #1 on the following pages. The worksheet is provided to help your understanding of what we have been studying together to merge into a discovery.

2. __Read__ the as yet unfinished chapters in your prior assignments from "The Family" by John Bradshaw. If you are current in your reading, please use this time to go over discoveries you have made in the last three sessions. Make notes on the questions that rise as you read. .

3. At some point during the week, before the next class session, please consider the comparison chart you made on the Worksheet, in question 14. As you look at the ages listed next to unmet bonding needs in your life, take a few moments to __Connect__ the relationships and situations that apply to that particular bonding need. These instances, as well as the bonding need listed will serve as clues in helping you to get your heart open in learning to accept and receive the love of God; thus enabling you to become a relational person.

Relational Living -- Worksheet #1 (3)

Look back now, over your answers to the Clue Questions for the past three sessions. Let's pull those answers together and see if we can't garner a fresh perspective.

From Session One –

1. How does God view the tendency to operate alone, not relating or sharing life?

   _____

2. Was living in relationship with others part of God's original design? _

3. Does God want to have a relationship with you on a deep level? _____

4. Which of the following elements argue with your knowledge of God's desire for relationship? (mark all that apply)

    a. I am afraid God will abandon me
    b. I don't need a deep relationship. Things are fine the way they are.
    c. I should be able to figure this out on my own.
    d. I am afraid I will fail.
    e. What if the promises don't apply to me?
    f. I am waiting for something to happen to change things.

5. Which of the following seem difficult for you when it comes to relating to others? (mark all that apply)
    a. knowing my feelings
    b. knowing what to say
    c. relating without anger
    d. feeling imposed upon by those around me
    e. having a desire to be with people (wanting to get away, be left alone)
    f. not feeling good enough
    g. relating without defensiveness
    h. understanding those around me

From Session Two –

6. Look back over your answers to Clue Question #5. Copy the areas you circled in answer to that question here.

7. Transfer the written statement from Clue Question #6, that most closely describes your experiential relationship with God, as well as the number you circled.

8. Considering the Levels and Stages of Personal Development on page 32, and Clue Question #7, where do you feel you are living your life on an IQ (or cognitive) level?

        a. birth to 2 years
        b. 3-7 years
        c. 8-12 years
        d. 12 years to adult

9. Considering the same chart on page 32, and Clue Question #7, where do you feel you might be living your life on an EQ (or emotional development) level? *(If you are unsure as to where you might be living, ask a trusted friend or colleague who knows you well for their insight.)*

      a. Stage 1
      b. Stage 2
      c. Stage 3
      d. Stage 4
      e. Stage 5
      f. Stage 6

Copy the description of the stage you circled from the chart on page 32, here.

10. On page 34, please review the indicators you made regarding your ability to feel, from the "Levels of Attachment and Moral Conscience Development" chart. Below, make an average, generalized estimate as to where you are living overall in regard to the goals of a bonded person in the last column. (To clarify the goals, re-read the descriptions on pages 36-37).

```
        0     1     2     3     4     5     6     7     8     9     10
    Unbounded                      some impairment              well-bonded
    and unattached                 and difficulty in            deeply bonded
                                   attachment
```

Make extra notes here:

11. With which life-orbit did you most identify?_____ Is this orbit

open or closed in nature?_____.

12. Which life-orbits oppose your personal goals and present themselves most readily?
_____

13. Which elements of self-defense create difficulty for you, and sabotage your efforts, when you try to move more relationally in your life? (See box in chart on page 45).

14. From your answers to Clue Question #14, transfer your observations to the columns below. In the third column, make a note, based on the chart on page 48, as to which area of living the need presents itself (whether IQ or EQ), and the age at which its fulfillment is necessary.

Fulfilled bonding needs		Unmet bonding needs	IQ/EQ & age

Session Four – "Open? Or Not?"

What we will learn in this Session:

We will learn the difference between a closed and open life-orbit, and what those represent in our ability to relate to other people. We will discuss the five levels of love relationship outlined in the Scripture, and see how the relational structure of our family of origin helped in developing our personal life-orbit, and our own ability to invest our lives in relational living. We will address additional situations and influences which further hampered our ability to trust. We will discuss the necessity and practice of an open life-orbit pattern, and how to develop the Discipline of Open-ness. We will tie those discoveries to the calling of Jesus to Intentional Discipleship.

Added to the class is an Emotional Maturity Worksheet, and a Physical Bonding/Substitution Principle chart for the student's personal usage for assessment and discovery.

The Instructor's Goal for this Session:

To provide the student with concepts for assessing road-blocks perhaps heretofore unrealized in relational living. To ready the student for discussion sessions as the class moves forward with the healthy goal of living in relational community in mind.

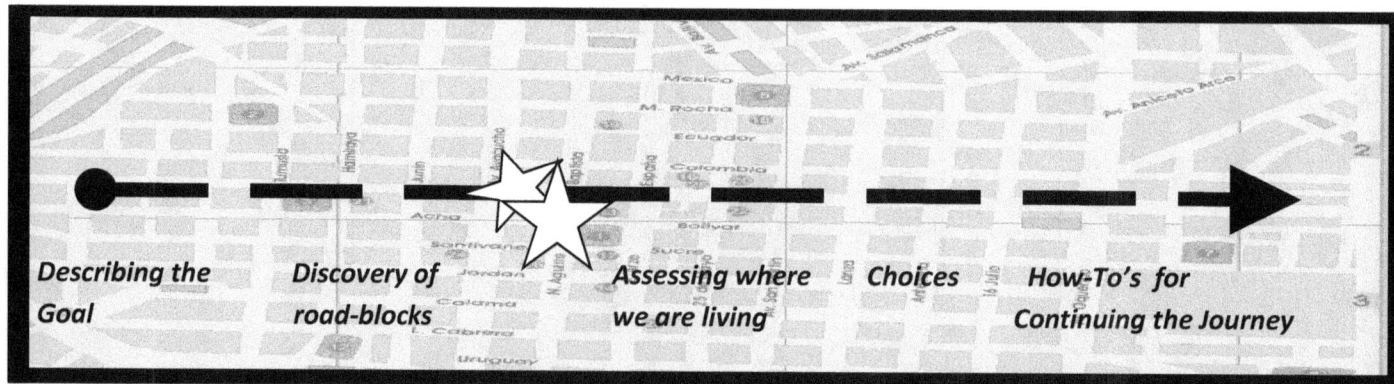

Session Four –
"Open? Or Not"?

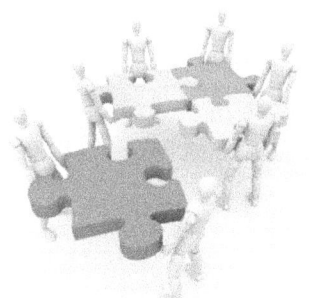

Let's Review

Relational Principle #1 –
Human beings are inherently self-centered, without ability or capacity to give or receive love outside of relationship with God, because <u>God is love</u>. Jesus Christ is God.

Relational Principle #2 –
Spiritual development and emotional maturity are intricately connected and cannot be separated. Growth in these areas of life happens inter-dependently

Relational Principle #3 –
Our experiences, imprintings and relationships in early life development are catalysts for our deep perceptions and core beliefs regarding ourselves and how life works. Elements that have hindered healthy living are destructive and must be addressed, owned and healed.

Clue Question #15-(4)

Imagine you are listening to a friend who describe their current difficulties in their relationships. Considering the above three relational principles, and the discoveries you have made so far, what changes would you suggest he or she make in how they approach and respond to the people in his/her life?

> *In our growth/journey to become mature in our personal discipleship, we will experience battle within the soul (mind, will and emotions) between these three personal life-orbit patterns.*

Motivated by Self-Approval. A self-centered orbit is the natural (untouched by God) order. It is the basis of narcissism, and a closed orbit. *(Closed)*

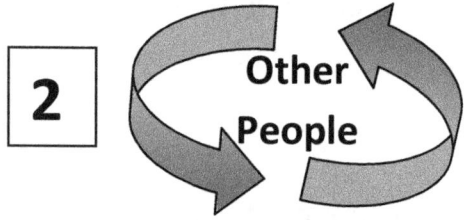

Motivated by Man's Approval. A people-centered orbit is the natural (untouched by God) imitation of God's order. It is the basis of inverted narcissism, or co-dependency. *(Partially closed)*

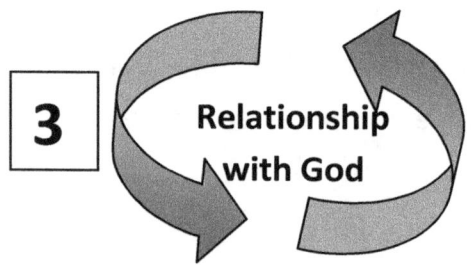

Motivated by God's Approval. A God-centered orbit is the super-natural (touched by God) order of the Spirit-formed believer. It is the life of the intentional disciple then the bond-servant. *(Open)*

Clue Question #16-(4)

Looking at these three life-orbits, consider the relationships you would most like to see become healthy in your life – think about how you find yourself responding and reacting to those particular people... Where might you have the wrong center-of-orbit? Write your thoughts here.

Human Core Desires

IQ (head, intellect)

1. Cliches   (to be "normal")   to be acknowledged (complimented, praised)
   To be noticed (seen)

2. Facts   (to "matter")   To be seen (recognized, remembered)
   To be physically safe
   To be included
   To be affirmed

EQ (emotions and sense of self)

3. Values, Principles (male)   To experience safe touch
   Morals and Feelings (female)   To be heard
   To belong
   (to be "in the group")   To be received

4. Needs and Yearnings   To be emotionally safe (and secure)
   (to be "at home in all   To be chosen ("first pick for the team")
   settings")   To be understood (sense of connection)
   To be included
   To be trusted

Sense of Belonging And Sense of Being

---

5. **Inner Child -- Core Union**   To be chosen (worth waiting for)
   (usually within marriage – can be a   To be safe (without fear, no need to hide)
   David/Jonathan relationship)   To be trusted completely (no sense of rejection or
   (to have something unique   disapproval)
   to offer/ to serve well)

Relational Principle #4 –
We cannot give away what we have never received.

Clue Question #17-(4)

Looking at the chart above, mark the core desires you find difficult to consider in others. You might even be unaware, or observe those desires/needs to be unimportant and ballooned by others to unreasonable proportions. Write those here.

Five Levels of Love Relationship

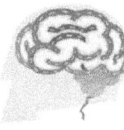

1. "Phileo" --- friendship

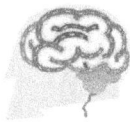

2. "Storge" – caring concern

- -

3. "Storge" w/"Agape" – unconditional love

4. "Agape" – selfless love

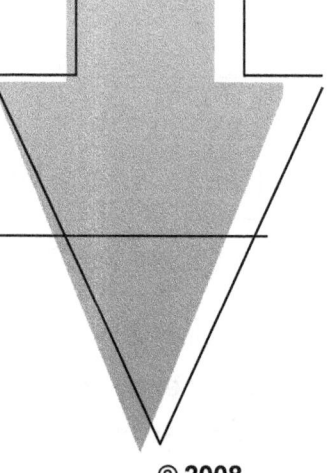

5. "Yada" (Heb) – Core Union
   "Ginosko"- (Greek)

Depth of Emotion and Commitment

© 2008

Family Diagrams

*Note: Father God's plan and purpose for family life is a safe and secure place; emotionally, physically, and spiritually for each family member. Family Life is a God-created environment where Design and Destiny can be discovered, encouraged, developed and pursued with purpose. While Marriage is a Place **where intimate relationship is developed** between a man and woman who have chosen each other for a life partnership, Family Life is a place **where the children are to be developed** and allowed to grow, encouraged by the parents.*

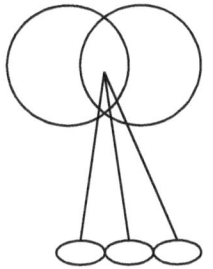

Healthy Family
Father and Mother have learned to operate together, and present decisions and options to children together, as a unified team. Children are ministered to on an equal basis, with no favoritism shown or expressed. **Focus: Abba's plan for the common good.**

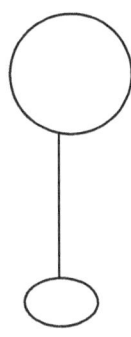

Healthy Single Parent Relationship
Each parent has learned to connect with the child's inner person, and can communicate from a relational point of view future goals and discipline. **Focus: Abba's plan for the common good.**

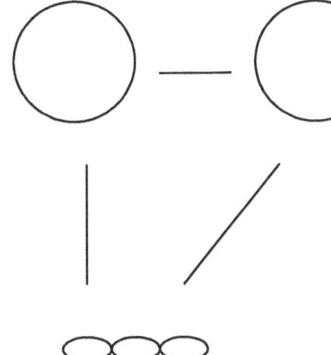

Unhealthy Parent Relationships
Parents are unconnected with each other and with the children. Communication takes place regarding task and fact levels only. Children receive communication, but there is no connection. Result: children receive a sense of abandonment and isolation, and become task oriented for approval. There is little or no affection communicated. **Focus: Personal rights, needs and/or appetites.**

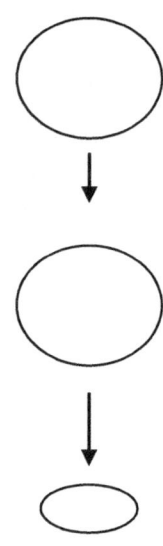

Authority Driven Model (unhealthy)

One parent is seen as having all authority, and communicates with the children through a chain-of-command, without personal relationship with the child. The child is distanced in the relationship and has no opportunity to appeal or question decisions. Voice and Identity are diminished within the family, for all members except the family member with the most authority.

Also within this model, one parent must continually explain the other to the child. The parent in the explaining role tends to lose personal identity and become co-dependent, seeking to keep peace in the home at any price. Acceptance is performance oriented. **Focus: To succeed on all fronts. To meet expectations**

The Abuse Model

The parents have experienced relational failure in their own abilities to build a marriage. They are emotionally distanced. Communication regarding the relationship is made to the child, and the child feels they must choose between parents.

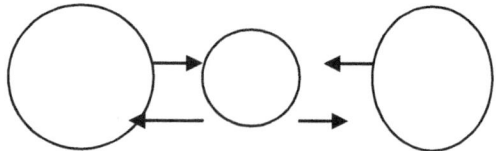

The child becomes the caretaker, and must meet the emotional needs of the parent; many times this involves verbal, emotional, physical, or sexual abuse (order of progression). The child must continually choose between parents, and perceives they must keep everyone happy. Identity development is stopped, and the child must choose an alternate "power" personality to survive. If a "power" personality is not found, the child will become depressed and lethargic. Approval is shame based **Focus: To survive**

The Island Model

The parents have experienced relational failure in their own abilities to build a marriage. They are emotionally distanced. There is no communication.

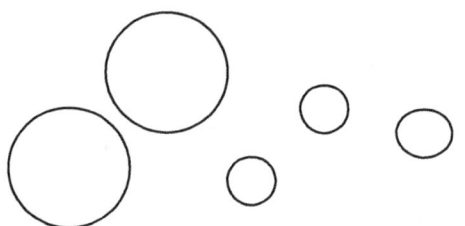

Everyone in the family lives in a separate environment. Everyone Is taking care of themselves, and no one is connected emotionally. There Is no care on mutual level. There are no bonding moments that can be remembered in this model **Focus: To survive**

Clue Question #18-(4)

What behavior model did your family of origin look like? (chart on pg 62-63) Using those provided diagrams as a template, create your own family diagram in the space below.

Relational Living -- Worksheet #2 (4)
Personal Gen-gram (core needs)

Clue Question #19-(4)

Which human core desires for bonding were not present in the family members you have drawn? Which family members or authority figures did not address your unaddressed/mis-addressed core desires?

These are the areas where you will struggle with an inclination to avoid relationship, to deny the need for relationship, feel a need to seek approval/perform for relationship, or even close to a self-centered or narcissistic life-orbit pattern.

Other Situations and Influences

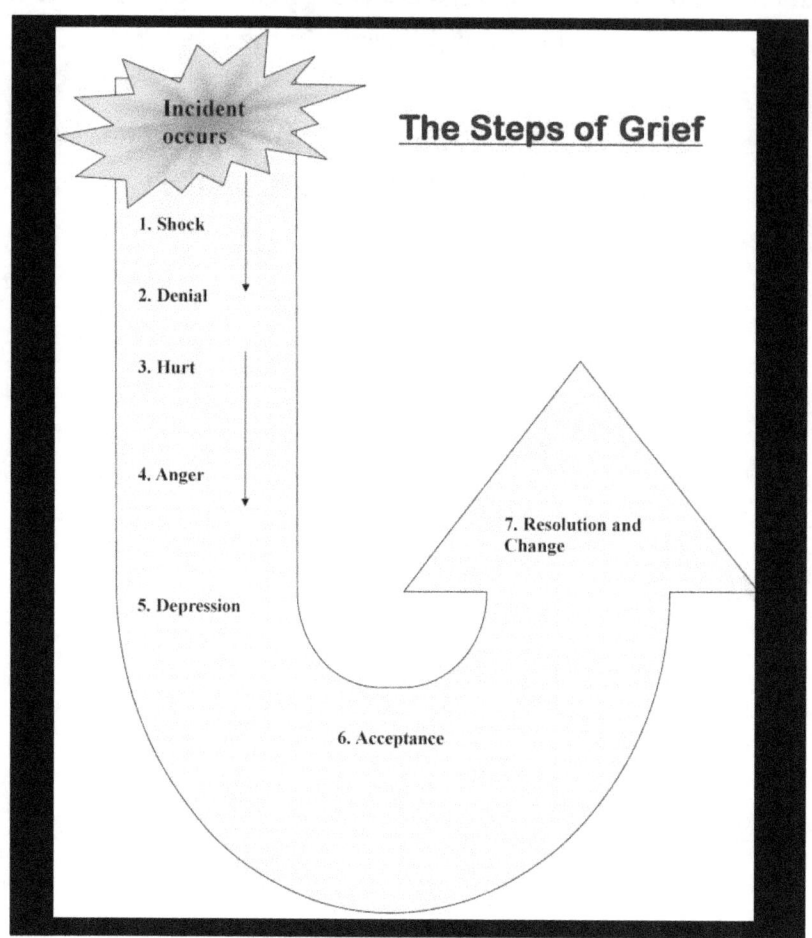

Notes:

Survival Mode and its Effects on Relationship

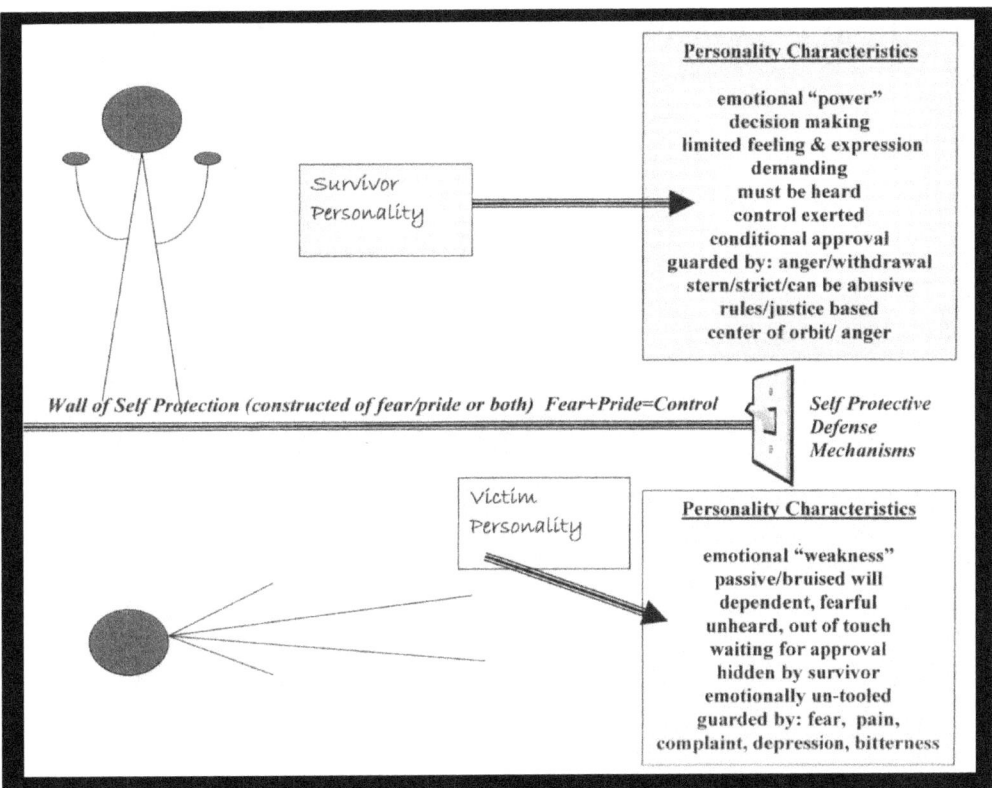

> **Note:** Shame, Grief (over losses and broken trust), and Pain are the areas of living where God desires to meet us and teach us what it means to become deeper in areas of living. When we close those areas of ourselves, or deny and ignore them, we stop growing in those areas, because we place our "self" in the middle of the orbit pattern.
>
> The patterns of Pain, Shame and Grief are actually the beginning places of development for the Intentional Disciple of Jesus Christ.

Notes:

Clue Question #20-(4)

What other situations and relationships come to mind, which might have caused you to avoid relationship? Write those people and circumstances here.

The Discipline and Practice of Open-ness

How does a Person's Life-Orbit close?

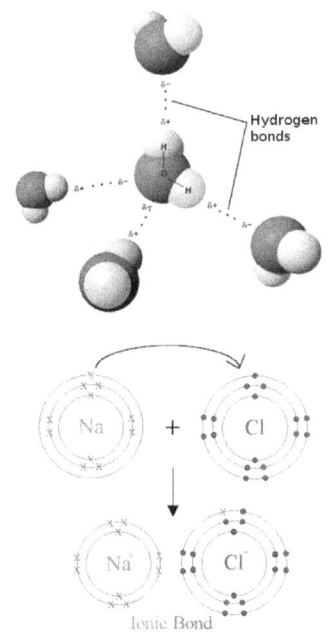

What enables us to receive?

How do we learn to bond?

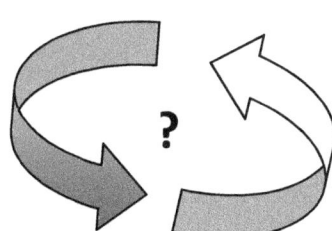

Johari window illustration.

At the beginning of a relationship

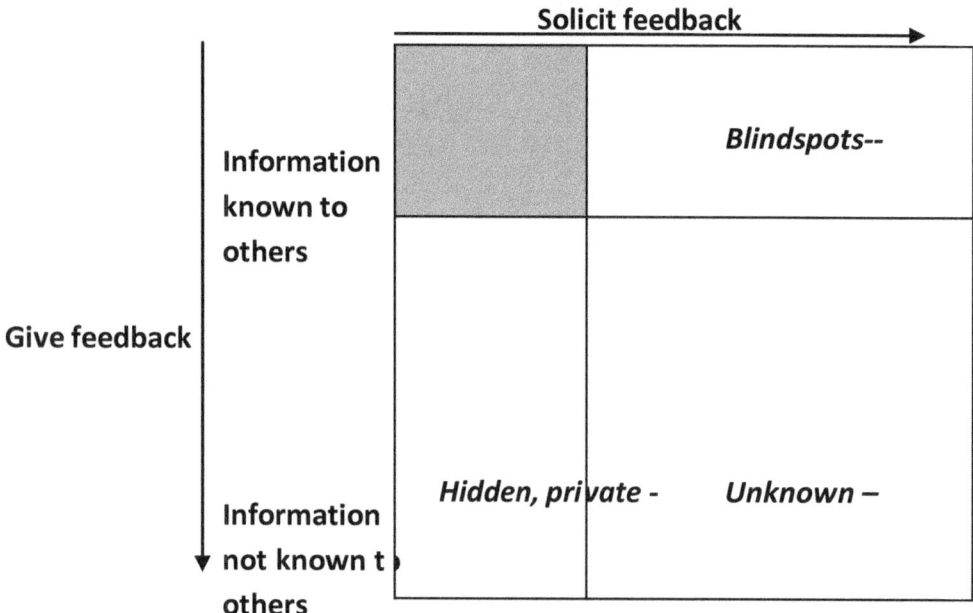

As the Relationship grows:

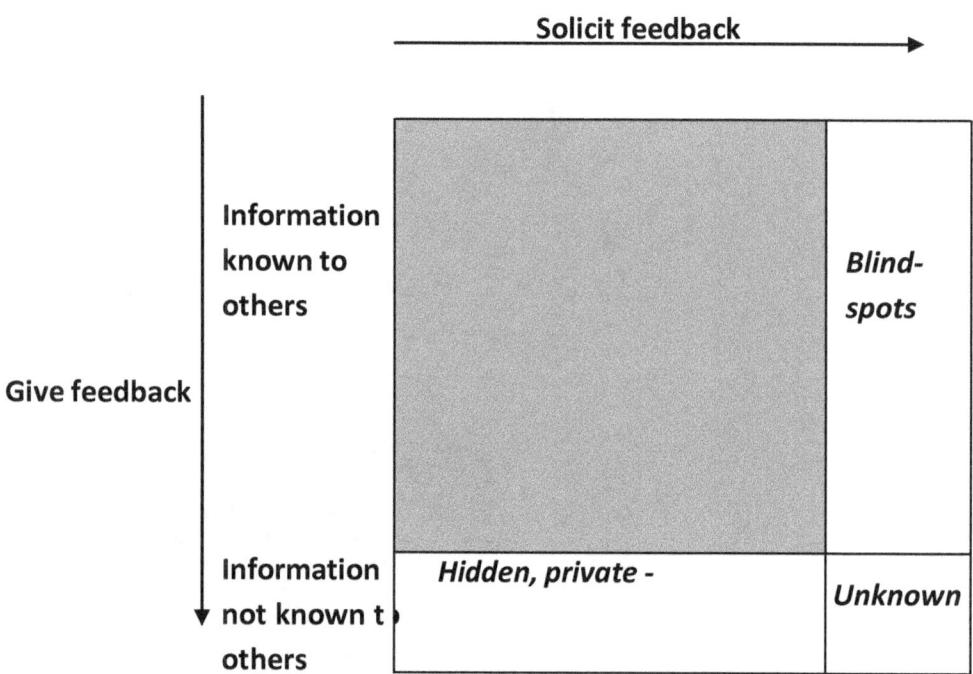

Clue Question #21-(4)

Are there relationships that have tried to "force" the splitting open of a closed orbit in your life? What happened to that relationship? Looking back now, what do you wish you had known?

Comparisons of Truths Learned So Far

IQ (surface only)	closed orbit	survivor	hard soil	no/little emotion	bonding impaired
EQ (heart of man)	open orbit	inner child	good soil	healthy emotion	relational

> Note: When Jesus Christ becomes the center of our life-orbit, we discover the beginning place of learning to become a disciple, or learner/follower. Discipleship is intentional, and involves several key elements.
>
> 1. The ability to tell ourselves "no."
>
> 2. The desire <u>to know</u> and then obey God; relationally, without fear of punishment. *We do this by developing an internal relationship with the Holy Spirit.* The first step of this relationship is personal surrender of our rights and attitudes.
>
> 3. Choosing <u>to adopt</u> and then <u>absorb</u> the goal of growing up into the nature of Jesus Christ. As a result, we find ourselves desiring to do the right thing, because it is the right thing to do; relating to other people in the way Jesus would, because His Spirit is speaking to us, and directing our lives.

Comparisons – A Carnal Believer to an Intentional Disciple

Jesus said to His disciples, "If anyone desires to come after Me, let him deny himself and take up his cross and follow Me. For whoever desires to save his life will lose it, and whoever loses his life for My sake will find it." Matt 16:24-25

A Carnal Believer

1. Will unload about difficulty, but not apply change to learn
2. Will talk intention, with no follow through
3. Hates correction; when corrected makes no response
4. Inwardly angry when not perceived as perfect
5. Resists counsel – has a stanced repulsion to difficult/hard truth
6. Has to be placated or persuaded before agreement happens
7. Sees themselves as an exception
8. Status minded
9. Tells you why truth doesn't apply to them, in their situation
10. Blames other people or circumstances for their own lack of change or growth
11. Is offended by the challenge to change
12. Wants to figure it out without help; has to appear "okay"
13. Only receives help (minimally) when desperate
14. Sees personal achievements and goals as the reasons for pursued development
15. Selective in relationships
16. Must remain at surface level to survive (Peter Pan syndrome/*male & female*)
17. Must make a good presentation
18. Wants to understand *before* they obey (no trust)

Inner Life Litmus Test for Life Approach –

"If I am happy, comfortable, and agree with my station, then everything is good."

An Intentional Disciple

1. Asks questions of leaders to apply truths to struggles
2. Follows through on intention, even at personal cost
3. Asks for, and applies correction
4. Openly admits imperfections, and asks for help to grow
5. Applies difficult truth; aligns with counsel
6. Sees personal need; dialog happens without argument
7. Sees themselves as a part of a whole
8. Steps into rank without posturing
9. Welcomes and applies truth
10. Accepts personal responsibility
11. Chooses and welcomes challenges to change because those challenges represent growth.
12. Practices intentional open vulnerability with mentors and teachers
13. Realizes need for help on all levels
14. Development is pursued because Holy Spirit is the focus of life pursuit
15. Relationships happen on the basis of spiritual connection and spiritual life
16. Personal goal is to grow "into the full stature of Christ."
17. Must have obedience as reputation
18. Obedience happens *because* they trust

Inner Life Litmus Test for Life Approach –

"Is my Passion for Jesus the most important thing in my life?" "Is the Presence of God filling and surrounding my life today?"

The Journey Into Healthy Discipleship

Jesus said to His disciples, "If anyone desires to come after Me, let him deny himself, and take up his cross and follow Me. For whoever desires to save his life will lose it, and whoever loses his life for My sake will find it." Matt 16:24-25

Levels of Communication		Territory of a Carnal Believer	In Community Life	In Life Approach	Inner Life Litmus Test for Life Approach –
1. CLICHES (I.Q. – head)	↑	1. Blind 2. Insensitive 3. Unaware 4. Nurtured/Bolstered Pride	1. Defends self first – Without real vulnerability 2. Must be "right" 3. Justice centered 4. Comparison driven 5. Image focused	1. Trusts self most 2. Standard for truth is relative to comfort level 3. Intellectually driven 4. >Few close relationships	*"If I am happy, comfortable and agree with my station, then everything is good."*

Line of Self Preservation – reinforced by perceptions of truth and life approach beliefs

		Territory of An Intentional Disciple	In Community Life	In Life Approach	Inner Life Litmus Test for Life Approach –
2. FACTS (I.Q. – head)					
3. VALUES/FEELINGS / MORALS (E.Q. – heart)	↑	1. Has eyes open/learns 2. Senses/Hears the Spirit of God 3. Aware of personal life effect/ diligent obedience 4. Intentional humility (authentic)	1. Listens and Receives correction; asks questions Honest vulnerability 2. Takes responsibility 3. Relationship centered 4. Obedience driven 5. Growth focused	1. Trusts Jesus most 2. Standard for truth is the Word of God/inner witness 3. Father's purpose driven 4. Opens life to others	*"Is my Passion for Jesus the most important thing in my life?"*

Line of Life-long commitment (Picture of Christ and the church)

		Territory of a Bond Servant	In Community Life	In Life Approach	Inner Life Litmus Test for Life Approach –
4. NEEDS and YEARNINGS (E.Q. – heart)					
5. MARRIAGE/ CORE UNION IQ and EQ on both sides of the relationship	↑	1. Passionate to maintain condition of heart 2. Honest communication w/Spirit 3. Lives by eternal values 4. Worked-in humility	1. Repents first – Asks for correction 2. Resolves w/Truth 3. Relationship centered 4. Holy Spirit led 5. Growth focused	1. Trusts Jesus most 2. Standard for truth is the Word of God/inner witness 3. Empathy driven 4. Relationships are God provided for His purposes	*"Is the Presence of God filling and surrounding my life today?"*

Clue Question #22-(4)

Study the charts on pages 71 and 72, regarding "The Journey Into Healthy Discipleship." On each chart, mark areas where you can recognize your own behaviors in your spiritual growth. Make a note here – where do you see yourself living – in IQ or EQ? Where has your response to personal pain and difficulty stopped your spiritual growth?

Do you like living in this place? Are you fulfilled in relationships?

What goals (from these charts) do you see that would be helpful to be addressed in your growth and living patterns?

Emotional Maturity Worksheet

As we discover and grow in our mind and emotions, we move into deeper levels of emotional maturity. How is it possible to tell where we are living? Is it possible to become emotionally mature? Consider the following questions:

1. Do you make and keep commitments?
2. Could you live on your own and take care of yourself?
3. Are you even-tempered and peaceful?
4. Do you have the skill and desire to cope with change?
5. Can you make decisions with reason rather than emotions?
6. Do you have effective communication skills? Do others in your life understand you?
7. Do you accept responsibility without being reminded or pressured?
8. Do you see other people as valuable even when you are in conflict with them?
9. Do you perform a job well because you have respect for yourself and value of following through?
10. Can you give up short-term comfort for long term gain?
11. Can you solve problems skillfully?
12. Do you set your own goals and are you self-motivated to reach them?
13. Are you sympathetic and responsive to what others need?
14. Are you confident about your ability to handle whatever comes your way?
15. Can you set aside your own needs when someone else's needs are more important?
16. Are **you** controlling the direction your life is taking, or are you passively allowing situations to shape your future with no personal initiative?
17. Are you able to feel positive emotions more than half of the time?
18. Do you maintain control of your emotions most of the time, without denying them?
19. Do you have a strong and positive sense of who you are created to become?
20. Do you expect your life to turn out well, even though you might have difficulties?

A person who can truthfully answer yes to most of these questions is likely to have a more developed sense of emotional maturity. Emotional development is the most crucial element in learning to become a relational person.

Bonding Worksheet – Physical Touch (Substitution Principle)

1. Eye to Body	Noticed Complimented	**IQ** **Cliché**
2. Eye to Eye	Seen and appreciated	**IQ**
3. Voice to Voice	Included	**Facts**
4. Hand to Hand	Safe touch (non sexual)	**EQ**
5. Arm to Shoulder	Understood	**Values**
6. Arm to waist	Accepted/Approved	**Feelings**
7. Face to face	Emotional safety	**EQ**
8. Hand to Head	Belonging	**Needs**
9. Hand to Body (safe touch)	Trusted	**Yearn**
10. Mouth to body	Completely secure	
11. Hand to genitals	To be held safely	**CORE**
12. Genitals to Genitals	Known and completely understood without rejection	

Clue Question #23-(4)

Consider the questions you answered in the Emotional Maturity Worksheet on page 74. Now look at the Physical Bonding sheet above. Where have you substituted physical bonding (sexual activity) for emotional connection?

> ### Relational Principle #5 –
> When we become aware of our needs to bond, incremental choices and actions are required to begin/continue the connection/bonding process. Bonding does not "just happen."

Clue Question #24-(4)

Consider the statement in Relational Principle #5, above. What discoveries are you making regarding your ability to relate to others, and the reasons why you relate the way you do? Write those discoveries here.

This Week:

*1. **Journal** your answers to the eleven questions presented in the class materials. Please think through your answers. Take a little time this week to consider how what you are learning, and what you have discovered about your own life patterns fit together with your level of spiritual maturity.*

*2. **Read** chapters 7,8 and 9 from "The Family" by John Bradshaw. Make notes on the questions that rise as you read. .*

*3. As you have time this week, look through the materials from the past four sessions. Prayerfully ask the Holy Spirit to make real to you (help you grasp the necessity and the "want-to") the areas of your life where He is calling you to live more relationally. The materials we have studied so far have hopefully provided you with tools to discern the areas where your spiritual life and emotional life are in need of personal attention. At some point during the week, create a "you are here" description as best you can, to mark the beginning point of relational discipleship. Ask the Holy Spirit to **Connect** what you see now, to the place where He wants to develop and take you in maturity. Doing this will help you to remain encouraged to keep your heart open; and in continuing to accept and receive the love of God; thus enabling you to become a relational person.*

Session Five – "When God is in the Middle"

What we will learn in this Session:

We will assess our personal discoveries so far, and begin the process of assessing where we are presently living in our ability to relate to others well. We will learn the difference between Judgment and Assessment, and discuss God's principle of Meditation/Agitation. We will learn in what ways all human beings are the same. We will learn how our inner thoughts regarding ourselves and others have affected our self-concept. We will utilize the materials disclosed so far to discover where we are in the Heart-Relational Ability- Recovery Process.

We will learn how Relationships Evolve, and see the pathway ahead. We will take a quick look at the study materials added to this session, regarding the inner road-blocks of Pride, Fear and Control, to aid the student in learning how to change their Inner Life orbit pattern, where needed. Finally, we will address possible missing puzzle pieces in our personal Life Experience history, and see what ingredients might be missing in our understanding of how healthy relationships/family work.

The Instructor's Goal for this Session:

To help the student begin the process of personalizing the materials studied so far. To open discussion for the class, for connection and discovery. To provide a safe environment where difficulties can be assessed without fear of judgment or disapproval.

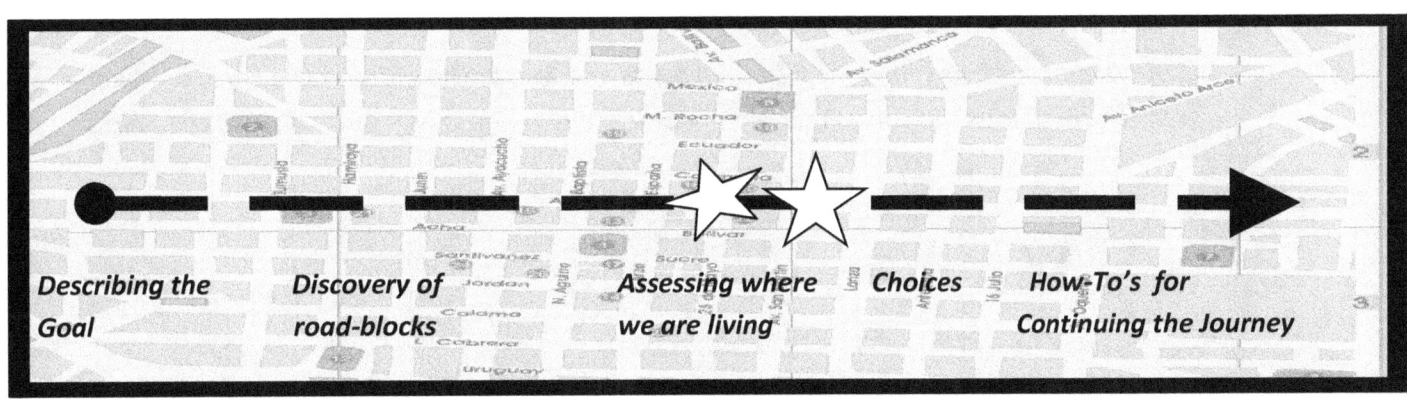

Session Five

"When God is in the Middle"

Let's Review

Relational Principle #1 – Human beings are inherently self-centered, without ability or capacity to give or receive love outside of relationship with God, because <u>God is love</u>. Jesus Christ is God.

Relational Principle #2 – Spiritual development and emotional maturity are intricately connected and cannot be separated. Growth in these areas of life happens inter-dependently

Relational Principle #3 – Our experiences, imprintings and relationships in early life development are catalysts for our deep perceptions and core beliefs regarding ourselves and how life works. Elements that have hindered healthy living are destructive and must be addressed, owned and healed.

Relational Principle #4 – We cannot give away what we have never received.

Relational Principle #5 – When we become aware of our needs to bond, incremental choices and actions are required to begin/continue the connection/bonding process. Bonding does not "just happen."

> *"But we all, with unveiled face, beholding as in a mirror the glory of the Lord, are being transformed into the same image from glory to glory, just as from the Lord, the Spirit."*
> *II Corinthians 3:18*

Personal Discoveries made to date:

1. Where do you see yourself living in emotional development?   IQ   or   EQ

2. What type of soil (parable of the sower and the seed), do you perceive you are living within your ability to relate to the Word of God, the Holy Spirit, and to other people?

IQ	roadside
	Shallow, no root
EQ	distracted, choked
	Good soil: 30/60fold
Core	100 fold

3. To what level of bonding, do you feel secure and confident to invest your life in relationships?

   1. IQ--Cliches   (to be "normal")
      - to be acknowledged (complimented, praised)
      - To be noticed (seen)

   2. IQ --Facts   (to "matter")
      - To be seen (recognized, remembered)
      - To be physically safe
      - To be included
      - To be affirmed

   3. EQ-- Values, Principles (male)
      Morals and Feelings (female)
      - To experience safe touch
      - To be heard
      - To belong

      (to be "in the group")
      - To be received

   4. EQ--Needs and Yearnings
      (to be "at home in all Settings")
      - To be emotionally safe (and secure)
      - To be chosen ("first pick for the team")
      - To be understood (sense of connection)
      - To be included
      - To be trusted

   5. Core --**Inner Child** --
      (usually within marriage – can be a David/Jonathan relationship)
      (to have something unique to offer/ to serve well)
      - To be chosen (worth waiting for)
      - To be safe (without fear, no need to hide)
      - To be trusted completely (no sense of rejection/ disapproval)

4. What relationships are most difficult for you to develop and maintain?

| Authority figures | Men | Women | Teenagers | Children |

| Family | Strangers | Working Environments | Church Based | Neighbors |

| Teachers | Doctors | Police | Lawyers | Imposed/unrequested |

5. Consider the bonding ages indicated on page 44. Where would you estimate yourself to be living emotionally (age level), and needing to begin in the process of pursuing relationships?

6. Consider Kohlberg's levels of Emotional Development on page 29. Which level seems most comfortable to you in regard to living your life day to day?

7. Where do you find yourself living most regularly?

Others centered	Self centered	God centered
(Fear focused)	(Pride focused)	(Love focused)
()	()	()
Needing man's Approval	separating giving self-approval	Intentionally relational/community

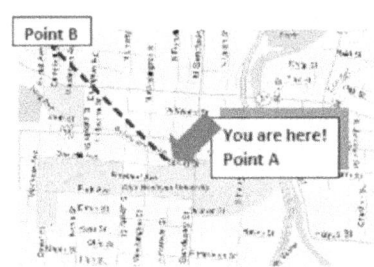

Assessment

Point B – Health
Point A – Present Location

Before a pathway can be charted to a final destination of health and development, we must assess or appraise where we are presently living. Without a proper appraisal, it is impossible to map out a straight line; creating personal application of the need for growth.

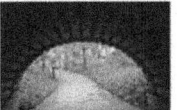

Results:
Truth/reality speaks
Emotional awareness
Healing of memories
Grief is processed
Facilitates growth and healing

Judgment

Good or Bad
Pass or Fail
Right or Wrong
Win or Lose

Judgment attaches a *negative moral value* to the "You are Here" mechanism and closes the gate to growth/change.

Results:
Negative emotions speak/control
Numbness of heart
Repressed memories
Stalled grief cycle
Stops growth and healing

© atg/dcg

Notes:

Assessment	Judgment
"GOD IS MY HEALER AND FRIEND"	*"GOD IS A HARD MAN, WAITING FOR ME TO MESS UP"*
Abba Father views us through the eyes of assessment, seeing our places of pain as potential meeting places for comfort and healing.	We view ourselves through the eyes of judgment, seeing our places of pain as places of potential rejection, disapproval and ultimate rejection by God.

Elements of Assessment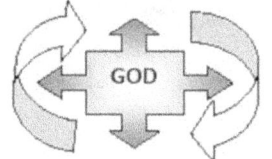

Elements of Judgment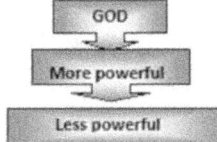

Assessment

1. Assigns value to people because they carry the image of God within themselves – either with Jesus or without Him.
2. Operates through a heart choice of love, trust, community, and mutual safety.
3. Uses potential and relationship to motivate; Holy Spirit led, serving based; Kingdom order.
4. What a person does flows from who they are becoming
5. Weakness and mistakes are expected elements of learning
6. Abba Father based, relationship centered
7. Acceptance and approval are centered in the unconditional and unfailing love of God—all are equal.

Judgment

1. Assigns value to people based upon beauty, achievement, Success, health, brains, and ability
2. Operates through a mindset of authority, hierarchy, politicism, religious traditions & institutional organization.
3. Uses fear to motivate; performance driven; man's order
4. What a person does is more important than who they are
5. Weakness and mistakes diminish value /unacceptable
6. Man based; Rules centered
7. Rejection and disapproval of those who are different than Common group

© atg/dcg

Notes:

The Meditation/Agitation Principle

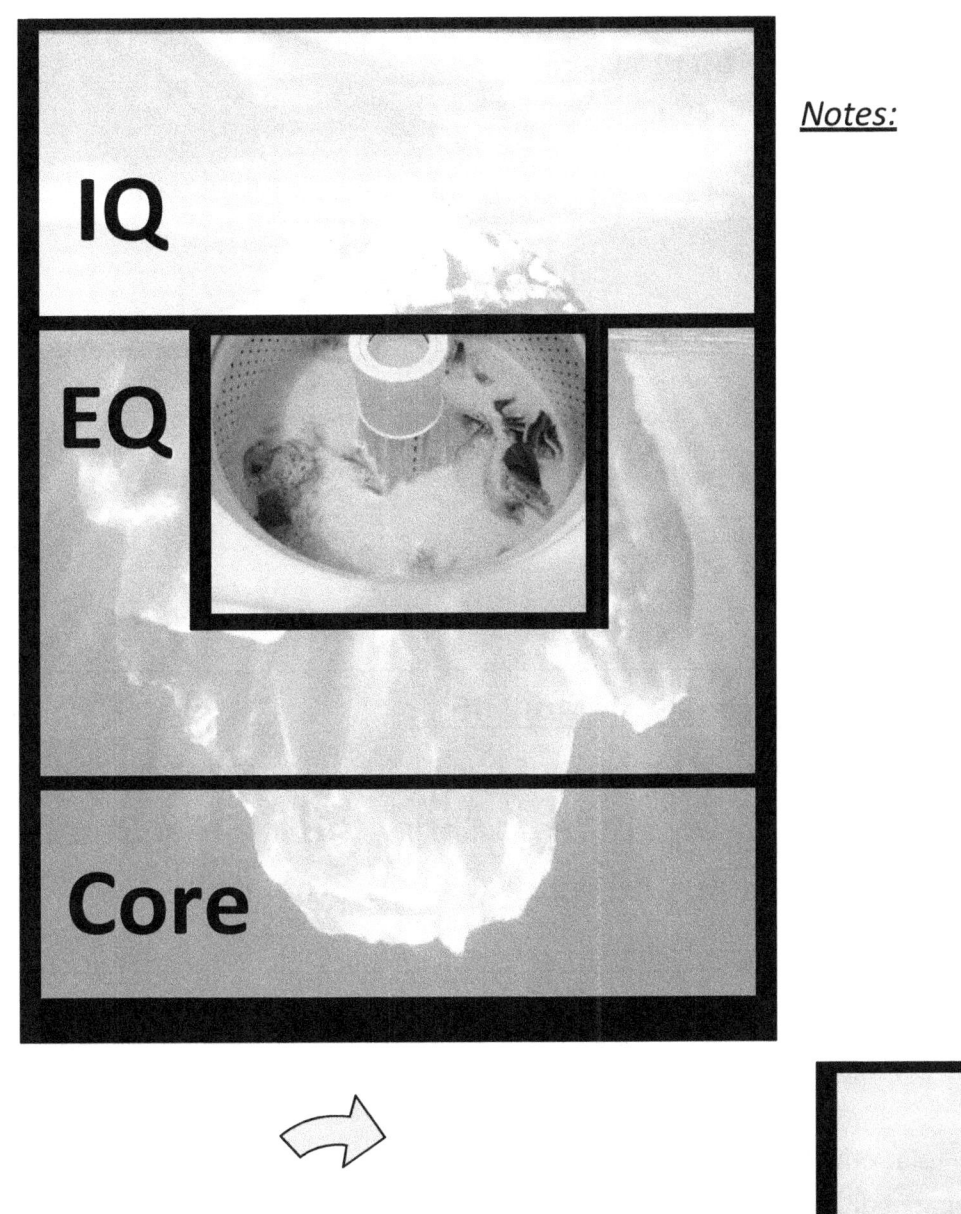

Notes:

or

When we say "yes" to a Self-Orbit, we say "no" to a God-Orbit.

Clue Question #25-(5)

"Bonding gaps in childhood become love needs in adult life." Are there bonding gaps that have prevented close relationships in your life? List them here.

Thinking about it now, how do they resurface (Meditation/Agitation Principle) in your relationships?

Relational Principle #6 –

Connection, Bonded-ness and Attachment cannot be achieved without intentional pursuit. For the follower of Jesus Christ, this is a requirement for healthy discipleship and community (Body-Life).

Clue Question #26-(5)

Consider the statement in Relational Principle #6, above. How does this principle affect your attitude towards maintaining healthy relationships in your life?

The Art of Bonding – The Restoration of Relationship

"Do unto others as you would have others do unto you."
Matthew 7:12

Everyone wants to feel "normal"
Everyone wants to be complimented
Everyone wants to be noticed
Everyone wants to be seen
Everyone wants to be remembered

Everyone wants to be included
Everyone wants to experience safe touch
Everyone wants to be heard
Everyone wants to be "in the group"
Everyone wants to be emotionally safe

Everyone wants to be emotionally and secure
Everyone wants to be "at home everywhere"
Everyone wants to be understood
Everyone wants to be included
Everyone wants to be told they're worth waiting for

Everyone wants to have no need to hide
Everyone wants to be completely trusted
Everyone wants approval
Everyone wants to have something unique to offer
Everyone wants to be able to serve well

Everyone wants to be acknowledged
Everyone wants praised
Everyone wants to matter
Everyone wants to be recognized
Everyone wants to be physically safe

Everyone wants to be affirmed
Everyone wants to feel important
Everyone wants to belong
Everyone wants to be received
Everyone wants be picked first for the team

Everyone wants to be understood
Everyone wants to be chosen
Everyone wants a sense of connection
Everyone wants to be trusted
Everyone wants to feel valuable

Everyone wants to live freely, without fear
Everyone wants to live free from rejection
Everyone wants acceptance
Everyone wants to know when they have done well
Everyone wants to be someone's confidant

The easiest part of becoming a relational person is realizing that we all have the same emotional wants and needs.

Results of Early Bonding Experiences

	THOUGHTS OF SELF	
	Positive Connections	Negative/Absent Bonding
Positive Imprinting & Modelling	++ **Secure and comfortable With intimacy, Communication, and Autonomy**	+- **Preoccupied with earning approval, and relationships**
Negative Encounters & Lack of Modelling	-+ **Becomes Dismissive of intimacy, strongly Independent**	-- **Fearful, shy, avoids intimacy & socially avoidant**

THOUGHTS OF OTHERS (row label, left side)

Notes:

Consider: Where are you living Emotionally?

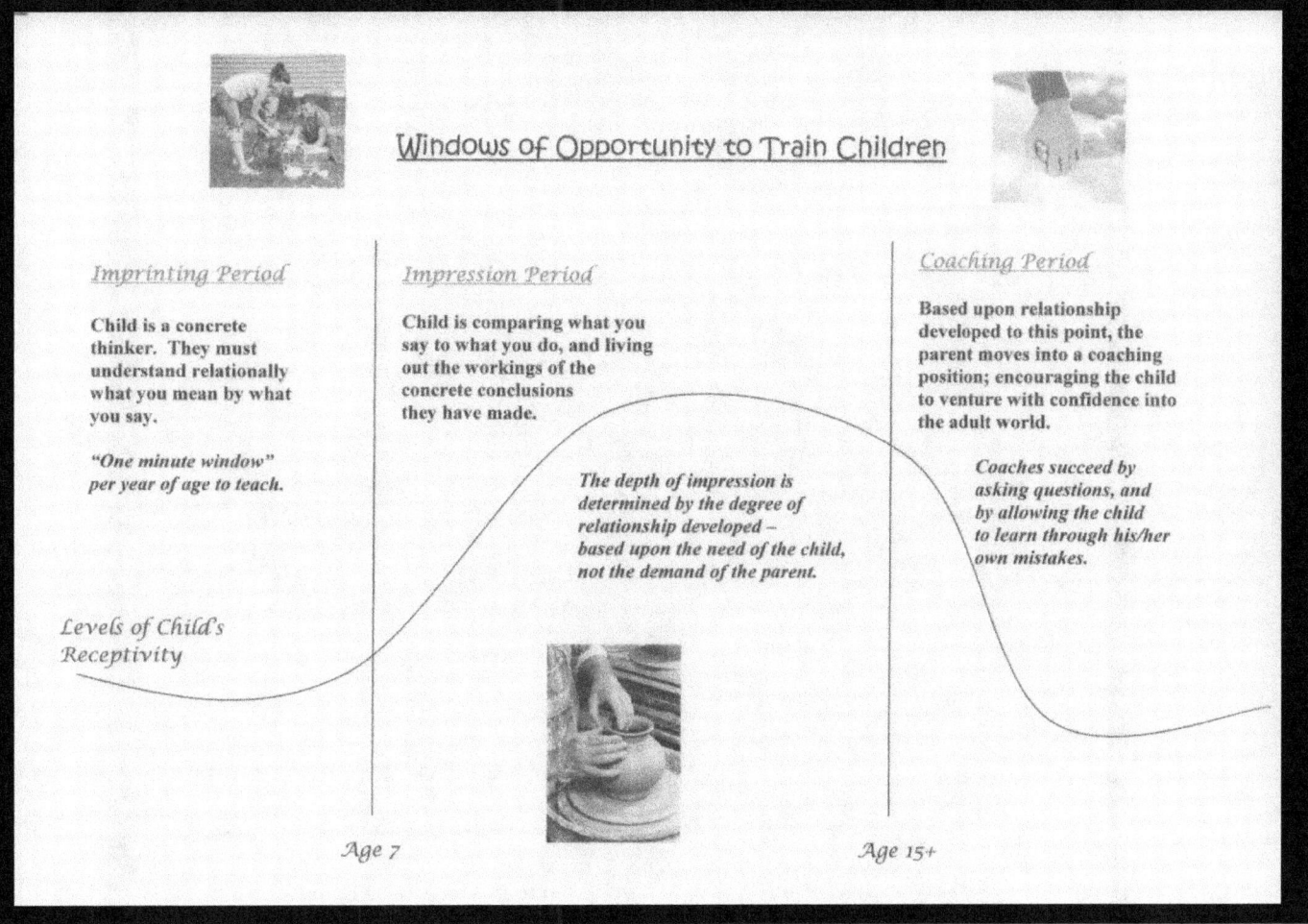

Notes:

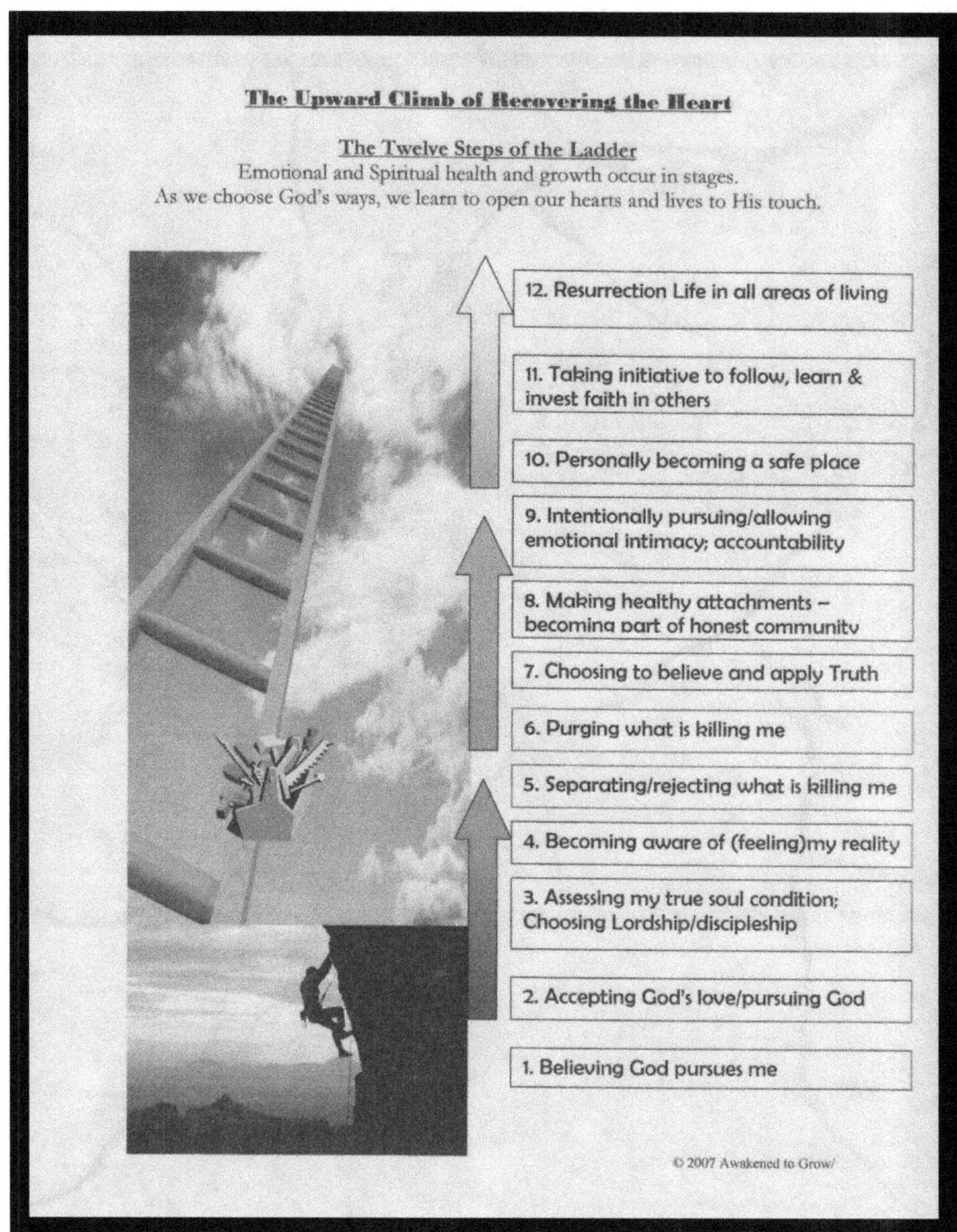

Notes:

How Relationships Develop

1. Attraction and Beginning

Stage one – As two people notice each other, they realize a mutual acceptance between them. There is some anxiety, as well as anticipation, as each considers how to develop relationship. Communication is made on a cliché and facts level, as they try to develop emotional boundaries of understanding, learning to read each other's signals.

2. Anxiety and Battle

Stage two – As relationship continues, there inevitably occurs conflict; in varied strengths and depths of emotion. These conflicts will occur in areas where emotional tooling has not been provided for each individual. When conflict is realistically resolved, and not ignored, the relationship deepens in emotional intimacy ("into-me-see") and the foundation for trust is established.

3. Acceptance and Belief

Stage three – As the pattern for conflict resolution is deepened, and communication is also deepened, trust and genuine unity are formed. Loyalty begins to be developed, and pain is shared.

4. Action and Blameless

Stage four – As relationship and trust are built upon, through experiences, shared pain, and communication, it becomes a natural next step to seek the best for the other person. The relationship can bear weight. Heartfelt serving occurs. Dreams and hopes are shared. Values are common. Feelings are validated. True safe community comes into the experience of relationship. Others people are included in the relationship.

5. Adjust and Belong

Stage five – As unity and trust have been developed, a weaving of identities has occurred, creating safe community. This is a safe place for healing, wholeness and growth to take place. Accountability is based upon the depth of relationship, and each person's attention to personally providing safety and encouragement for others. Fears are shared, validated and worked through. Feelings are faced with companionship and support. Genuine care is provided.

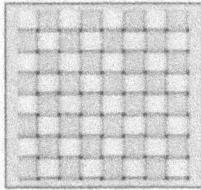

© 2008

Notes:

Relational Principle #7 –
There are no short cuts to building depth in relationship or in the process of maturity.

Clue Question #27-(5)

Consider the statement in Relational Principle #7, above. What does this statement mean to you in your present understanding of how Life and Relationships work?

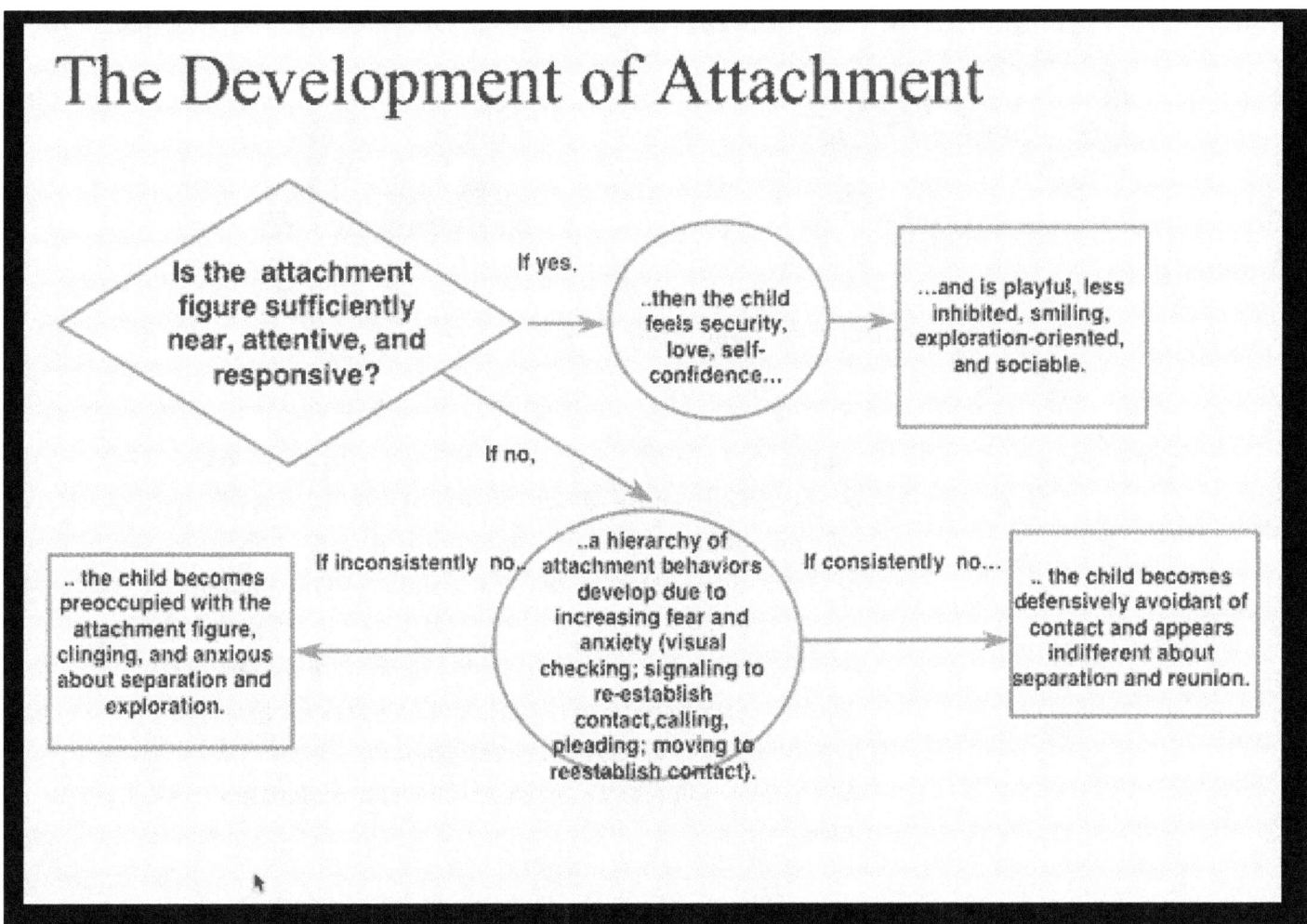

Notes:

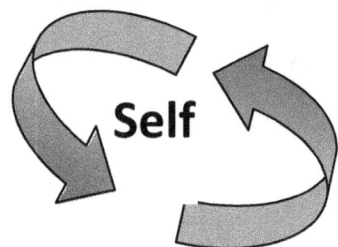

The Blindness of Pride

(the root of the self-centered, or narcissistic orbit)

II Corinthians 4:3-4   *But even if our gospel is veiled, it is veiled to those who are perishing, whose minds the god of this age has blinded, who do not believe, lest the light of the gospel of the glory of Christ, who is the image of God, should shine on them.*

I John 2:10-11   *He who loves his brother abides in the light, and there is no cause for stumbling in him. But he who hates his brother is in darkness and walks in darkness, and does not know where he is going, because the darkness has blinded his eyes.*

Pride, simply put, is the unwillingness to allow God to protect and take care of us.

Qualities of Pride – Pride refuses to acknowledge or admit need. Pride makes comparisons, presumes, rebels and seeks to be independent, while at the same time, demanding that everyone in its sphere of influence come into its way of thinking. It will not associate in vulnerable community. It blames, criticizes, and places its own opinion above anyone else's. It is the root of selfishness, placing its own needs and wants above those of anyone else. It seeks to be understood, rather than to understand. It seeks to rule. It seeks to control. It demands to be heard. In its most raw form, it is denial. In its inverted form, it takes the form of self-pity, victimization, and accusation, continually stating that it has been misunderstood.

All demonic torment has its root in pride.

James 4:6   *But He gives more grace. Therefore He says: " God resists the proud, but gives grace to the humble."*

Phrases Pride Will Not Say , or Finds it Difficult to see the need to say –

1. **I was wrong. Dead wrong."** (without accompanying explanations or excuses.)

When humility makes this statement, it does so without explanations or excuses. It also admits truth. Jesus wants us to live in the truth.

Psalm 15:1- 2   *LORD, who may abide in Your tabernacle? Who may dwell in Your holy hill? He who walks uprightly, and works righteousness, and speaks the truth in his heart;*

Ephesians 4:15   *that we should no longer be children, tossed to and fro and carried about with every wind of doctrine, by the trickery of men, in the cunning craftiness of deceitful plotting, but, speaking the truth in love, may grow up in all things into Him who is the head— Christ—*

Psalm 51:6   *Behold, You desire truth in the inward parts, and in the hidden part You will make me to know wisdom.*

III John 1:2-4   *Beloved, I pray that you may prosper in all things and be in health, just as your soul prospers. For I rejoiced greatly when brethren came and testified of the truth that is in you, just as you walk in the truth. I have no greater joy than to hear that my children walk in truth.*

2. **"I am responsible."** (without accompanying rationalizations and blame).

When humility makes this statement, it does so without seeking to be understood. Rather, it seeks to make things right, and bring restitution.

James 4:6   *But He gives more grace. Therefore He says: " God resists the proud, but gives grace to the humble."*

3. **"I am willing to experience the consequences of my actions. I have earned them."** (without bringing justice arguments)

When humility makes this statement, it makes no comparisons with other's behaviors, or with regard to fairness. It is enough for the character quality of humility that the issues be settled on their on regard, without expecting others to facilitate or protect them.

Hebrews 12:5-6 *And you have forgotten the exhortation which speaks to you as to sons: " My son, do not despise the chastening of the LORD, nor be discouraged when you are rebuked by Him; For whom he LORD loves He chastens, and scourges every son whom He receives."*

4. **"I need Jesus."** (no self made solutions)

When humility makes this statement, it acknowledges its own need for Jesus, without making statements or judgments as to the behavior of others, or of their relational treatment. It seeks only to correct and make right its own person.

Psalm 10:4 *The wicked in his proud countenance does not seek God; God is in none of his thoughts.*

5. **"I can't fix myself."** (without knowledge arguments)
6. **"I don't know the answer."**

When humility makes this statement, it does so without making a defensive statement about what it knows, or what it has held on to as truth. I realizes that its needs help, and receives it willingly.

James 4:16-17 *But now you boast in your arrogance. All such boasting is evil. Therefore, to him who knows to do good and does not do it, to him it is sin.*

7. **"I trust God more than I trust myself, and that's wrong. I choose to trust God."** (without self reliance, or independence)
8. **"I surrender."**

When humility makes this statement, it recognizes personal need for accountability, discipline, and training. It recognizes that it is not its own authority, and opens observation those inner places of the heart where pride has ruled.

Jeremiah 49:16   *Your fierceness has deceived you, the pride of your heart, O you who dwell in the clefts of the rock, who hold the height of the hill! Though you make your nest as high as the eagle, I will bring you down from there," says the LORD*

Romans 9:19-21   *You will say to me then, "Why does He still find fault? For who has resisted His will?" But indeed, O man, who are you to reply against God? Will the thing formed say to him who formed it, "Why have you made me like this?" Does not the potter have power over the clay, from the same lump to make one vessel for honor and another for dishonor?*

9. **"I need to change."** (without self-defense)

When humility makes this statement, it stands in the place of security in the love of Father God, knowing that He will make things right, and that He will take care of how we are perceived, understood and known, as long as we stay in alignment with Him, and seek to keep our carnal flesh in check.

Proverbs 16:17-20   *The highway of the upright is to depart from evil; He who keeps his way preserves his soul. Pride goes before destruction, and a haughty spirit before a fall. Better to be of a humble spirit with the lowly, than to divide the spoil with the proud. He who heeds the word wisely will find good, and whoever trusts in the LORD, happy is he.*

10. "I repent. I was wrong. I'm sorry. Will you forgive me? What can I do to make things right between us?" (without self preservation attitudes)

When humility makes this statement, it receives and acknowledges responsibility for wrong behaviors, attitudes and treatments of others. It does not seek to hide behind a need to be seen as "right," or "in control."

II Corinthians 7:9-10 *Now I rejoice, not that you were made sorry, but that your sorrow led to repentance. For you were made sorry in a godly manner, that you might suffer loss from us in nothing. For godly sorrow produces repentance leading to salvation, not to be regretted; but the sorrow of the world produces death.*

11. "I need to be taught more than I need to be understood."

When humility makes this statement, it opens itself to others in a chain of command, asking those people to speak into the life for health and growth. It receives correction and teaching, and applies what it is taught, in order to bring about health and growth, and seeing change occur in the life.

Galatians 6:3 *For if anyone thinks himself to be something, when he is nothing, he deceives himself.*

12. "The truth is more important than anything I feel, or whatever image I portray." (with nothing to hide – no secret living)

When humility makes this statement it is acknowledging that the images we seek to portray are false, and that they never allow us to put God first. Humility is willing to live an honest life, without seeking to make impressions of success, achievement, financial status, or intellectual accomplishments. It is most concerned with straightforward relationships and honest living before God.

II Timothy 3:1-5 *But know this, that in the last days perilous times will come: For men will be lovers of themselves, lovers of money, boasters, proud, blasphemers, disobedient to parents, unthankful, unholy, unloving, unforgiving, slanderers, without self-control, brutal, despisers of good, traitors, headstrong, haughty, lovers of pleasure rather than lovers of God, having a form of godliness but denying its power. And from such people turn away!*

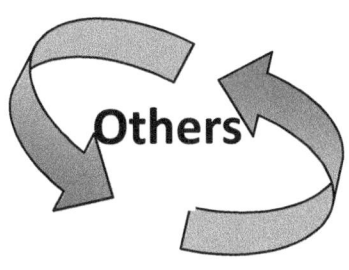

(the root of the others-centered, or inverted narcissistic/co-dependent orbit)

How To Expose and Break the Power of Fear

"For God has not given us a spirit of fear, but of power, and of love, and of a sound mind." II Timothy 1:7

"I heard the sound of you walking in the garden, and I was afraid, and I hid myself." (Adam to God) Genesis 3:10

1. A situation occurs, sometimes traumatic, which opens a door for fear and torment within the soul. Sometimes, the situation can take place over a period of time, such as the slow realization that an authority figure is unsafe. The circumstance is either re-lived, or is repressed, depending upon the person's ability to deal with it at the given time.

2. The wound remains open within the soul, and continually influences choices made in various life-areas. Eventually, it sends out "runners" within the soul that are evidenced as forms of fear.

3. Rather than deal with each attribute of fear, it is better to go after the memory, which is the legal ground the enemy has gained to torment the person.

4. Ask the Holy Spirit to reveal the circumstance. Repent for opening the door to the spirit of Fear, and for giving it place, by accommodating it. Renounce it's legal hold. Cut off generational ties to fear within the family, which have served to make it stronger, and have reinforced it's influence and ability to rule the life. Forgive those who were involved in exposing the person to Fear. Release the right to hold on the attributes of fear as part of the personality,. Apply the Blood of Jesus Christ. Anoint with oil, and break the yoke of bondage.

How Fear Takes Hold

"For God has not given us a spirit of fear, but of power,
and of love, and of a sound mind." II Timothy 1:7
"I heard the sound of you walking in the garden, and I was afraid, and I hid myself." (Adam to God)
Genesis 3:10

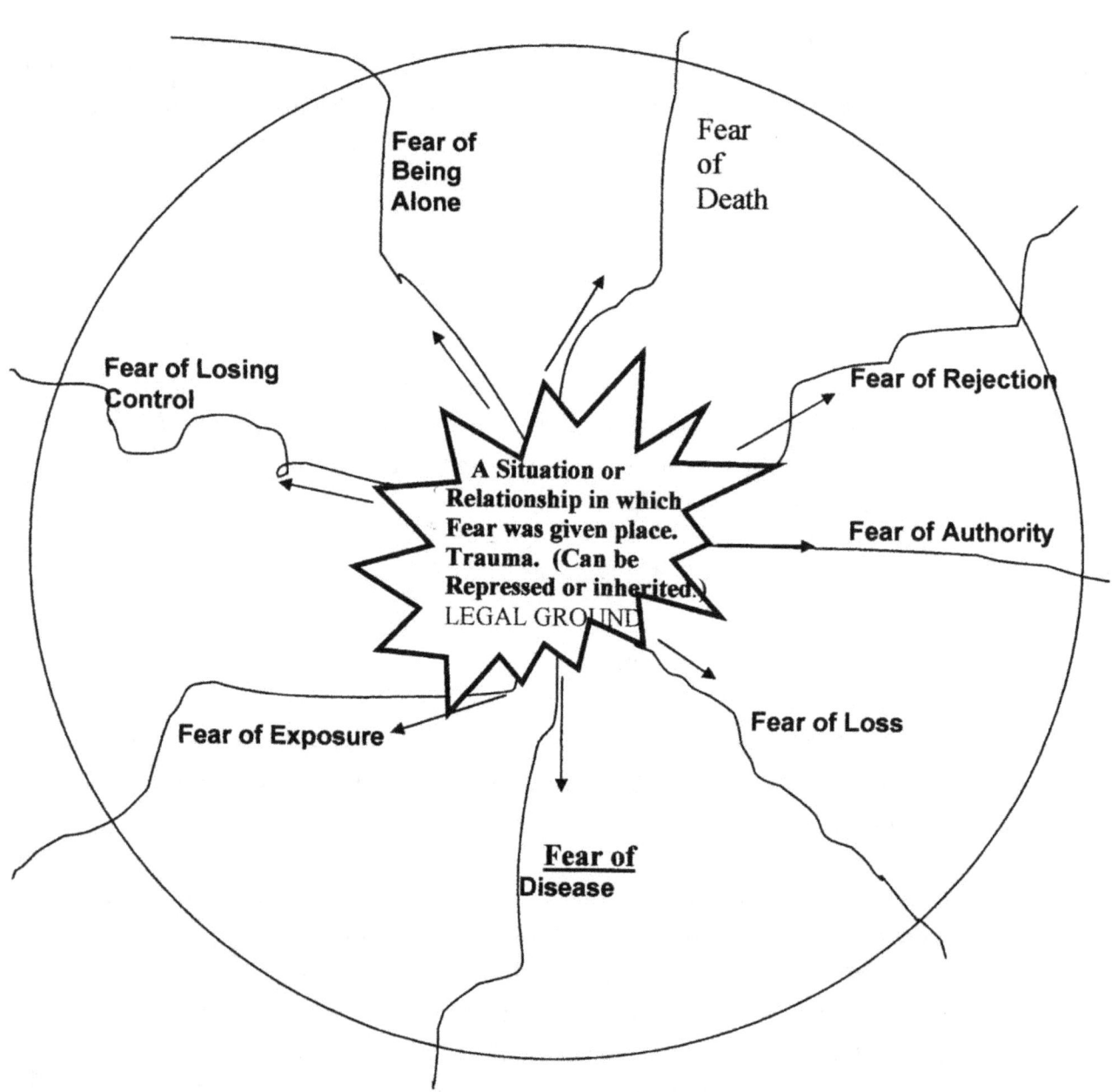

Qualities of Control (the combination of Pride & Fear)

Seeks to set criteria for acceptance and relationship
Feels it is owed due to what it feels it has given
Seeks to conform others to a given set of appearances
The spirit of Control has been known to use the following methods:

Overt Control
(Visible)
Examples:

Russian KGB
Chinese Communist Government
Military Surveillance

1. Imprisonment (emotional or physical)
2. Humiliation
3. Embarrassment (shame)
4. Coercion
5. Mandated communication
6. Bullying/Anger/Threats to cause regret
7. Invalidation, conditional validation
8. Spirit of disregard of a person's identity
9. Demanding information/must know
10. Seeking the limitation of others' through physical, verbal or emotional restraint

Subverted Control
(Under the surface)
Examples:

Spoiled Child
Crippled Grandmother
Image Consultant

1. Self Pity/ Pouting
2. Responding with Victimization/ Accusation
3. Guilt
4. Continual rehearsal of problem
5. With-holding of response—wants for other person to come to them.
6. Requiring persuasion or placation
7. Speaking for, or acting for another person without asking to know their heart
8. Blame/Communicated fear of loss of image
9. Creating indispensability
10. Manipulation of circumstance

To Abuse – *to use wrongfully, engage in hurtful practice, to destroy identity or inner life within an individual*

The Abuse Wheel

Note: 95% of all domestic abuse is targeted at the wife. For this reason, this chart refers to the abused as "her."

Power And Control

YELLING/SCREAMING Overpowering with volume and will when communicating
USING COERCION & THREATS Making and/or carrying out threats to do something to hurt your spouse * threatening to leave her, to commit suicide, to report her to welfare * making her drop charges * making her do illegal things

PHYSICAL VIOLENCE – any touch without permission used to gain agreement when communicating
USING INTIMIDATION Making her afraid by using looks, actions, gestures * smashing things * destroying her property * abusing pets * displaying weapons * invading her comfort zone and using your size to get her to yield

USING EMOTIONAL ABUSE
* Putting her down *Saying unkind things * Making her feel bad about herself * Calling her names * making her think she's crazy * playing mind games * humiliating her * having relationships with other women on trust levels that are designed to be for her alone *using guilt and shame to motivate her

USING ECONOMIC ABUSE
* Preventing her from getting or keeping a job * Making her ask for money *Giving her an allowance *Taking her money *Not letting her know about or have access to family income. *Not sharing your income, and keeping it for your own activities.

USING MALE PRIVILEGE
* Treating her like a servant, no household help with organization or chores – "provider mindset" *Making all the big decisions * Acting like the "master of the castle" *Being the one to define men's & women's roles * Spiritualizing the abuse, and calling it "submission." * Intentionally keeping her pregnant.

USING CHILDREN
* Making her feel guilty about the children * Using the children to relay messages * Using visitation to harass her * Threatening to take the children away from her.

MINIMALIZING, DENYING AND BLAMING
* Making light of the abuse and not taking her concerns about it seriously * Saying the abuse didn't happen * Shifting the responsibility for the abusive behavior * Saying she caused it, or she deserved it

USING ISOLATION
* Controlling what she does, who she sees and talks to, what she reads, where she goes. * Limiting her outside involvement * Using jealousy to justify actions.

SEXUAL ABUSE – Waking her up for sex; stimulation to bring response against her will
* Using her physical response to satisfy your own need, without regard for her emotions *Taking without giving lingering care or love-making *When sex is the only form of intimacy * Rape= sex against her will *Acting out Pornography *Forced abortion *Prostitution *Party sex

What areas of Power and Control were part of your past experience in life?

To Marry – *to trust another person with your life on a deep level, bonding to the point of the creation of a new and joint identity.*

The Healthy Marriage Wheel

EQUALITY in Relationship

ACTIVE LISTENING and NEGOTIATION
* Speaking kindly and with words that build relationship *Listening to each other's point of view without interruption or judgment, or defensiveness.

PARTNERING TO SEE NEEDS MET
* Seeking mutually satisfying answers to conflicts & disagreements
* Accepting and making changes
* Being willing to give ground.
* Not having to be "right," or have the last word.

BEING A SAFE PERSON –
Asking before touching, especially in areas pre-disposed to pain.

CREATING A SAFE PLACE --
Talking and acting in such a way that she feels safe and is comfortable expressing herself. *Inviting, without expectation, her participation in activities. * Being genuinely interested in what she feels and has to say.

RESPECTING HER
* Listening to her without judgment
* Being emotionally affirming and understanding.
*Being emotionally available
* Valuing her opinions, views and feelings.
* Allowing her to disagree with you, without becoming offended

ECONOMIC PARTNERSHIP
* Making money decisions together, viewing each one's viewpoint as vital and important.
* Being sure that everyone benefits from financial arrangements.
*Equally sharing and contributing earnings for the common good.

SHARING RESPONSIBILITIES
* Agreeing to and following through on a fair distribution of work in the home.
* Making family decisions together, as a team.
* Defining roles together, and being willing to help each other.
* Being truly spiritual, serving in the home as unto the Lord, with mutual submission

BEING A RESPONSIBLE PARENT
* Sharing parenting responsibilities equally
* Being a positive, encouraging, non-violent role model and mentor for the children.
* Bonding to the children

BEING HONEST And ACCOUNTABLE
* Accepting responsibility for your own actions
* Acknowledging your past usage of violence and/or abuse.
*Admitting being wrong, asking for forgiveness, making amends. Not repeating the abuse.
* Communicating openly and truthfully.

TRUSTING and SUPPORTING
* Encouraging her to follow her goals in life.
* Respecting her right to have her own feelings, friends, activities and opinions.
*Believing in her dreams and abilities.

SEXUAL HEALTH –
*Bringing identity issues into the light *Talking about needs and learning together, without demands.
*Mutually giving to each other, without fear.
* Honest communication regarding enjoyment
* More about giving love, than getting satisfaction
* More about emotional intimacy than body contact, stimulation or gratification

Which areas of Healthy Relationship were not addressed, and seem foreign to you?

To Parent – to bond with a child on the level of trust at a deep level, imparting life skills for independent development and trustworthy citizenship as a later adult.

Note: The responsibility for taking the initiation to bond in a parent/child relationship falls to the parent. It is action, born out of love and/or choice.

The Healthy Parenting Wheel

Healthy Parenting and/or Mentoring

ACTIVE LISTENING and NEGOTIATION
*Speaking kindly and with words that build relationship *Listening to the child's point of view without immediately correcting or criticizing.

PROVIDING TO SEE NEEDS MET
* Helping your child to resolve inner conflicts, through discovery
* Accepting and making changes
* Being willing to give ground.
*Not having to be "right," or have the last word, unless it is a safety issue.

BEING A SAFE PERSON –
Communicating safe touch, in safe areas, without invading privacy or comfort zone. Not intimidating a child, or threatening, even in silence.

CREATING A SAFE PLACE --
Talking and acting in such a way that the child feels safe and is comfortable in expression
*Inviting, participation in activities. * Being genuinely interested in what the child feels and has to say.

RESPECT
* Listening to the child without judgment— guiding with questions * Being emotionally affirming and understanding. * Discipline for child's inner life development; not because of personal frustration or embarrassment. *Being emotionally available * Valuing opinions, views and feelings. * Not being offended by disagreement, but seeking to teach for change.

ECONOMIC TRAINING
* Making money decisions together, teaching the child to manage earned money well, with tithing coming before purchase goals. .
* Teaching the child to be a giver, by modeling the example.
*Equally sharing and contributing earnings for the common good.

SHARING RESPONSIBILITIES
* Agreeing to and following through on a fair distribution of work in the home, teaching the child to work for rewards
* Allowing the child to contribute to family decisions when possible.
* Teaching the child to be a worker and a helper, not just to receive.
* Being truly spiritual, serving in the home as unto the Lord, modeling mutual submission.

BEING A RESPONSIBLE PARENT
* Sharing parenting responsibilities equally
* Being a positive, encouraging, non-violent role model and mentor for the children.
* Bonding to the children

BEING HONEST And ACCOUNTABLE
* Accepting responsibility for your own actions
* Acknowledging your past usage of violence and/or abuse.
*Admitting being wrong, asking for forgiveness, making amends. Not repeating the abuse.
* Communicating openly and truthfully.

TRUSTING and SUPPORTING
* Encouraging the child to discover their giftings, and to follow God-given goals in life.
* Respecting the child's own feelings, friends, activities and opinions.
*Believing in their dreams and abilities, and shaping values regarding Father's plan for those dreams.

SEXUAL HEALTH –
*Bringing identity issues into the light *Talking about needs and learning together, without demands.
*Answering questions the child asks without fear or avoidance, with honest appropriate for the age level.
* Allow child to see you hug and express care. Being willing talk about emotions.

Which areas of Healthy Relationship were not addressed, and seem foreign to you?

Notes:

This Week:

1. **Journal** your answers to the Clue Questions presented in the class materials. You can use the pages in this book to log your answers, or another journal. Please think through your answers. Take a little time this week to consider how what you are learning, and what you have discovered about your own life patterns fit together with your level of spiritual maturity.

2. **Read** chapters 10 and 11 from "The Family" by John Bradshaw. After you have finished reading the book, write a short paragraph about what you have learned. This practice enables your "head" and your "heart" to make connections. What have you learned so far? Try to put it into words..

3. **Utilizing the materials** we have studied to this point, try to determine which orbit presents itself to you when you feel a need to protect yourself. What have the lessons regarding that particular orbit alerted you to look for in as you relate to other people? What elements discussed in our classes so far are you realizing could present barriers in your ability to live relationally? Listing these potential barriers can help you not to be "blind-sided" by defense mechanisms, or strong emotions you weren't aware of. This type of intentional addressing of your concerns is essential if you are to deepen in the ability to live in a relational manner.

Session Six – "Choices: Starting Out Right"

What we will learn in this Session:

We will discuss the practical choices required in the process of becoming a relational person. We will address the how-to's of centralizing God into our life-orbit patterns, and learn the practical starting points for practicing healthy relationship. We will learn how our life-orbit affects our morality, our ethics, and our views of relationship. We will learn how to show others they have personal value, and what relationships are appropriate on each area of communication and relationship. We will discover the qualities of trustworthiness, and how to communicate that quality to others, enabling relationship.

The Instructor's Goal for this Session:

To equip the student with tools in developing a healthy understanding of how relationships work. To provide practical understanding of the bonding/attachment process. To mediate class discussion and discovery in a safe environment where difficulties can be assessed without fear of judgment or disapproval.

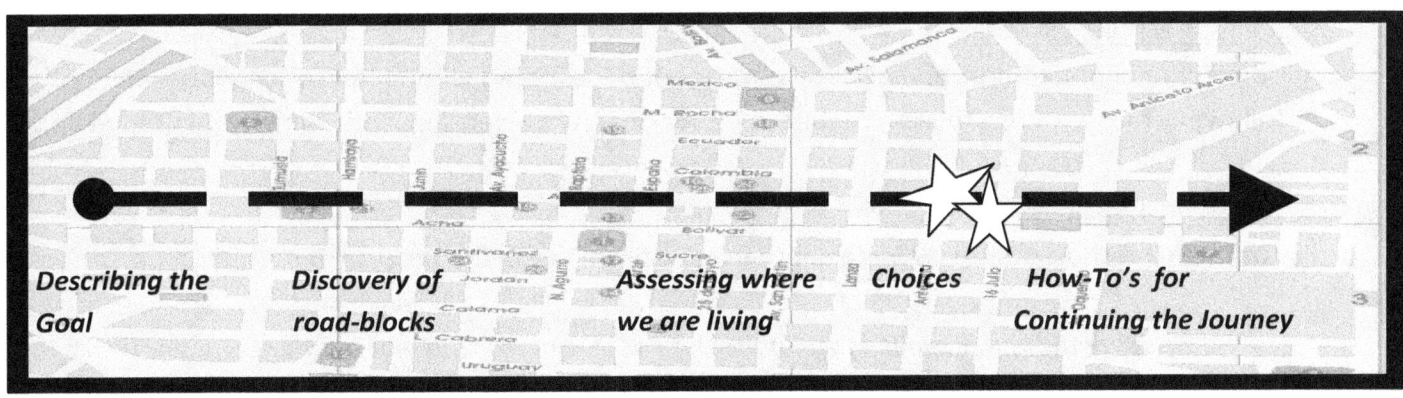

Session Six

"Choices: Starting out Right"

Let's Review

Relational Principle #1 – Human beings are inherently self-centered, without ability or capacity to give or receive love outside of relationship with God, because <u>God is love</u>. Jesus Christ is God.

Relational Principle #2 – Spiritual development and emotional maturity are intricately connected and cannot be separated. Growth in these areas of life happens inter-dependently

Relational Principle #3 – Our experiences, imprintings and relationships in early life development are catalysts for our deep perceptions and core beliefs regarding ourselves and how life works. Elements that have hindered healthy living are destructive and must be addressed, owned and healed.

Relational Principle #4 – We cannot give away what we have never received.

Relational Principle #5 – When we become aware of our needs to bond, incremental choices and actions are required to begin/continue the connection/bonding process. Bonding does not "just happen."

Relational Principle #6 –
Connection, Bonded-ness and Attachment cannot be achieved without intentional pursuit. For the follower of Jesus Christ, this is a requirement for healthy discipleship and community (Body-Life).

Relational Principle #7 –
There are no short cuts to building depth in relationship or in the process of maturity.

> *"But we all, with unveiled face, beholding as in a mirror the glory of the Lord, are being transformed into the same image from glory to glory, just as from the Lord, the Spirit."*
> II Corinthians 3:18

Clue Question #27 (6) –

Take a few moments to refer back to the Relationship Wheels on the closing pages of the last session. Transfer your answers here, from the questions at the bottom of each page.

Power and Control Wheel – what seems familiar in your past experience in relationships?

Healthy Parenting Wheel—which elements seem foreign to you; unaddressed, not experienced?

Healthy Marriage Wheel -- which elements seem foreign to you; unaddressed, not experienced?

Looking at these answers, consider: Those elements present on the Power and Control Wheel represent areas where you will be tempted to operate in a co-dependent/others-centered orbit, tending to become fear based, seeking approval, and tending to take control in the relationships you experience. The unaddressed/un-modeled elements from the Healthy Wheels represent areas where you will be tempted to operate in a closed orbit, tending to become self-centered, selfish, and filled with narcissism. In all of the wheels, those areas you have indicated will be areas where you will battle to believe that God could love you, or work a better solution in your life than you have experienced so far.

Would you like to be able to feel and ability to release these areas to God, and invite Him into the most intimate areas of your heart, changing the way you view relationship and therefore other people? Write out a prayer here.

Choice #1: Opening My Personal Orbit

Keys to Opening Your Own Orbit Pattern

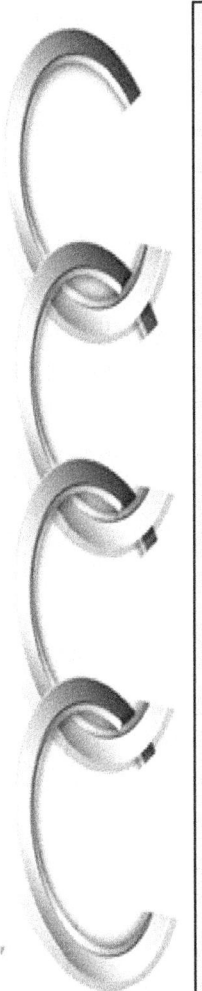

1. Realize that you were not designed to live your life alone (self-centered); nor were you designed to live your life in fear (others-centered). You were created and designed to be a relational person – first with God and then in community with others. Allow God to become your friend.

2. Although you have sought to do your best to live your life so far, take ownership of places where God has not been in the center of your orbit. Admit and own (to God, to yourself, and to others) that unhealthy patterns have influenced your choices in regard to relationships; specifically in how you habitually act and react. Ask God to help you to change.

3. Determine to relax and slow down in your responses; Realize that defense mechanisms actually prevent relationship, and prevent God and others from knowing who we really are. As best you can, take ownership of those defensive patterns you have used to survive emotionally. Ask the Holy Spirit to teach you and show you where you are using those mechanisms. Ask someone who is close to you emotionally (that means you trust them), to help you become aware when you are speaking and living defensively. (JoHari window principle)

4. Determine to release those who have hurt and injured you, causing you to become defensive. Let go of the desire to control how you are perceived and understood. Choose to live honestly with God and with others.

How Do We Begin to Become Relational?

Step One. We see ourselves as needing healthy relationships. It is not good for any of us to live our lives alone. We were created for community; first with God, then with others.

Step Two. We see the process of relationship from a healthy perspective. That healthy perspective then becomes our goal. Here is the healthy perspective: Our relationships are an eternal element in our lives that must be stewarded; nurtured, built, restored, kept healthy, given boundaries, and maintained. We recognize that healthy relationship can only occur if the Creator of the concept is part of the practice.

Step Three. We determine to trust God first for our development, rather than ourselves, or others. This is the releasing of pride. We ask God to forgive us for excluding relationship with Him from our efforts in relating to others, and invite the Holy Spirit of God into the process. We begin the learning journey of Inner Life Development, and Intentional Discipleship.

Step Four. We release those who have neglected, offended and wounded us, realizing our reactions to those offenses are the root and source for fear, shame, and control in our lives. If we have denied the grief we have experienced, seeking to survive, we open the door, and grieve our losses with God's help. We realize that this inner conflict is the road-block, or quick-sand, in our journey to become relational, and must be resolved.

Step Five. We allow God to meet us in our places of Abandonment and Pain, giving us His perspective on the choices of those who have damaged us. We accept and bond with His perspective, receiving His love and approval.

Reviewing Relational Principle #4 –
We cannot give away what we haven't received.
*(God becomes the Source to re-address
what we have discovered we are missing.)*

---

*"Everyone feels like they are on the outside,
until they put God in the center."*

Choice #2: Receiving God's Approval

The (Holy) Spirit of Adoption

"For you did not receive the spirit of bondage again to fear, but you received
the Spirit of adoption by whom we cry out, "Abba, Father.
The Spirit Himself bears witness with our spirit that we are children of God,
and if children, then heirs—heirs of God and joint heirs with Christ,
if indeed we suffer with *Him,* that we may also be glorified together."
Romans 8:15-17

Notes:

"Now I say *that* the heir, as long as he is a child, does not differ at all from a slave,
though he is master of all, but is under guardians and stewards until the time
appointed by the father. Even so we, when we were children, were in bondage
under the elements of the world. But when the fullness of the time had come,
God sent forth His Son, born of a woman, born under the law,
to redeem those who were under the law, that we might receive the adoption as sons.
And because you are sons, God has sent forth the Spirit of His Son into your hearts,
crying out, "Abba, Father!" Therefore you are no longer a slave but a son,
and if a son, then an heir of God through Christ." Galatians 4:1-7

Notes:

"Blessed *be* the God and Father of our Lord Jesus Christ, who has blessed us
with every spiritual blessing in the heavenly *places* in Christ, just as He chose us in Him
before the foundation of the world, that we should be holy and without blame before Him in love,
having predestined us to adoption as sons by Jesus Christ to Himself,
according to the good pleasure of His will,
to the praise of the glory of His grace,
by which He made us accepted in the Beloved." Ephesians 1:3-6

Notes:

Clue Question #28 (6) –
Consider the Healthy Relationship Wheels you referred to for the last question. These wheels represent and describe how our Heavenly Father deals with each of us in His relationship with us. In a family relationship like the ones these Wheels describe, would you be willing to trust Him as the Nurturing and Care-giving Father? Would you feel safe to accept His Values and System of Thinking?

Relational Principle #8 –
Honest vulnerability with God, self and others is necessary in order to maintain relationships, and learn to bond well. This is the "glue" factor for Community and Belonging.

Clue Question #29 (6) –
How does this principle apply to you in this new place of decision? Write out a short observation here.

Choice #3: Trade God's Value System for My Own
Comparison of Personal Values Thinking

 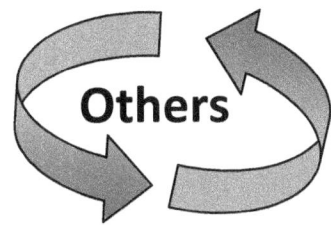 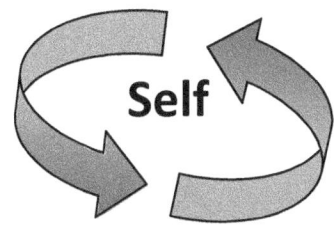

(based upon inner relationship With Holy Spirit/obedience Open/Depth of soul)

(based upon approval of other people/securing oneself through task and performance/conditional)

(based upon personal sense of comfort and satisfaction/ sets terms/ shallow)

"Servant-minded" (kinosis) Philippians 2 example

"Survival-minded" (protective) protective/shielding self

"Selfmade-minded" blinded/lone-ranger

1. Intentional disciple

1. Passive, needy

1. Stoic, has no need

2. Love-based (Agape)

2. Fear-based (reactionary, defensive)

2. Pride-based (unfeeling)

3. Operates within boundaries From relationship/ values others

3. Operates within boundaries in fear of rejection/judgment

3. Values boundaries when agrees with mindset

4. We value others because each person carries the image of God within themselves, whether positively or negatively

4. We value others when they contribute to our own sense of being useful, we become needed/essential.

4. We value others when they agree with our opinion; when they reinforce our own defense patterns.

5. We gauge our value by what God has said about us.

5. We gauge our value by the responses of others.

5. We gauge our value by how comfortable we are.

6. Our treatment of others is based upon the ethics described in God's Word.

6. Our treatment of others is based upon relative opinion, and our personal safety.

6. Our treatment of others is based upon our own desires, goals, & needs.

7. We live by absolutes, with the desire to communicate God's nature and comfort with others.

7. We live by relative absolutes, with the desire to be affirmed and encouraged.

7. We live by relative absolutes, with the desire to do as our appetites dictate.

When God is at the center, what is important to Him becomes important to us – our Heart-values change.

When God is at the center, we discover our value,
When we see our value, we can value others.

Note: It is impossible to relate well, attach, or
bond with anyone when they do not feel valued by you.

Choice #4: Show Others I Value Them, by Choosing to Become Relational

Actions	Words	Body Language	Tone of voice
Intentional Time	Listening	Serving	Prayer
Affection	Gifts	Encouragement	Gentle touch

Fifty Ways To Show Someone You Value Them

1. Ask a question about a project you know they are involved in.
2. Make an encouraging comment about a choice they have made.
3. Compliment them in the first 30 seconds of conversation.
4. Say something nice about them in front of another person.
5. Remember their name. Remember their birthday.
6. Help them focus on their strengths.
7. Be kind to them.
8. Help them to do something they are good at.
9. Write them a handwritten note, or letter.
10. Give them an unexpected gift.
11. Compliment/encourage one of their passions, or life pursuits.
12 Interest yourself in what interests them. Enter their world.
13. Smile at them. Honestly try to make them feel important.
14. Try to make them feel important. (honestly)
15. Practice good manners. Say "hello" to them. Say "please," and "thank you."
16. Take stock of how a person has added value to your life and tell them.
17. Try to do a little extra than is expected. (When you borrow a car, return it with the tank full.)
18. Budget time for them. Invite them to share an event with you.
19. Budget time for them. Become a listener.
20. Ask them: "Is there anything I can do for you?"
21 Try to connect them with others who could help them/enlarge their life experience.
22. Be a solution-speaker, rather than a problem-identifier.
23. Ask to hear their ideas; then share your own.
24. Make it your goal to serve them.
25. Make a decision to intentionally trust them – give them a chance at relationship.
26. Find areas of common ground. Develop them.
27. Laugh a lot. Help them see a bigger picture, from different perspectives.
28. Build time into your life to add value to others.
29. Make time for casual "hanging out."
30. Be open about your own weaknesses. This empowers others and helps them to trust you.
31. Try to see everyone you meet as they mean to be, rather than how they really are.
32. Affirm someone when they do the right thing.
33. Believe the best about them. Help them believe it too.
34. Be on time.
35. Respond. Don't react.
36. Be an example of right relationship.

37. Show respect, even of children. Be aware of your non-verbal communication. (actions, stance)
38. Develop a kind and happy greeting for meeting people.
39. Make it a practice to create memories.
40 Remember their special occasions. Remember their losses.
41. Be sincere. Share a secret with them. Keep a secret
42. Let them go first.
43. Don't expect someone else to see things your way. Try to see things their way.
44. Be observant of uniqueness. Be observant of effort.
45. Show interest in a relationship important to them.
46. Make eye contact. Remember someone's eye color.
47. Remember: Small people talk about themselves and others. Generous people talk about dreams and ideas.
48. Talk with people. Focus on the person you are talking with.
49. Communicate the things you are grateful for.
50. Choose to learn something from everyone; even if it is what not to do.

Clue Question #30 (6) –
In your present relationships, which persons need to experience a communication of validation from you – right now?

Which of the methods listed in the prior list would you like to try?

Healthy Rules for Bonding in Communication

(follow these four rules in every relationship, and bonding will happen every time.)

1. Be honest
(Speak the Truth with yourself, and with others.)

2. Take responsibility
(Admit when you are wrong. Listen completely.)

3. Be kind
(Value the other person's viewpoint.)
(Don't blame or accuse. Use gentle words.)

4. Wait your turn.
(Listen completely, without interrupting. Don't "groom" or "tweak.")

Notes:

Bonds of Attachment
In Relationships

IQ

1. Common Activities
2. Common Friends

EQ

3. Social bond – agreement Inner Person Affection/(Loyalties)
   Common Life Goals   Long Term History

4. Mutual Care (Two-way-nurturing) Communication styles (Investing of Trust)
   Sense of Safety

Core

5. Secrets (Confidentiality and security)   Spiritual bond- equal yoke
   Sense of Security

**Physical/Sexual Attraction can distract and substitute for
Genuine emotional intimacy on any level. Chemical attraction and
Gratification then become the focus of time spent together.**

Clue Question #31 (6) –
What discoveries are you making regarding the differing layers of relationships? How would you like to become deeper in your ability to relate?

Choice #5: Developing the Habit of Healthy Trustworthiness/Safety

The Process of Trusting – How it Happens

Over the past 100 years, innumerable studies have been done regarding the sensitive issue of Trust. Why do we trust? What are the emotional elements in a relationship that create a sense of Trust?

Based on consistent findings, here are some hints towards learning the art of trust; of investing yourself in a relationship, and helping someone else learn to trust you. Trust, in more than 99 out of 100 cases, is based on expectation. Apparently, to the degree you believe you can expect a certain response from someone, you trust that person. To the degree you believe that person will reciprocate at some point in the future in some (often undefined) way, you invest trust. Of course, past experience, whether with that same person, or with others, affects our confidence as well.

Here are some more clues to help in the trust process:

1. Experience. The more contact you have with someone, and the more you know about them, the more confident (trusting) you will be in what you expect from them.

2. Similarity. We tend to be more trusting of persons who are like ourselves. If someone looks, dresses, or acts as we do, we are more likely to expect them to also reflect our personal values.

3. Patterns. The more someone behaves with consistency, the better you're able to establish patterns and form expectations.

4. Respect for time. If someone is consistently punctual, it not only signals consistency, but also general conscientiousness toward other people.

5. Flexibility. Social-exchange theorists have found that people are more likely to trust someone who does not try to explicitly negotiate or force a binding agreement. (Think of the last car salesman you encountered.)

6. Confidentiality. The ability to keep a secret and exercise good judgment inspires trust.

7. Honesty. We want someone to keep *our* secrets, but not their own. Self-disclosure builds trust.

8. Competence. In the workplace, nothing inspires trust more than getting something properly, and doing it well.

9. Active Involvement. Trust is based on an understood reciprocity. If someone does not even appear to invest in you, he likely doesn't have much to lose in betraying you.

10. Personal Contact. Part of engaging is an effort to make "face time." A recent study showed people in the workplace are more likely to trust fellow workers with whom they interact in person more than those they work with via email or by long distance..

11. Eye contact (but not too much). This is perhaps the biggest behavioral indicator of trustworthiness. But the quality of the eye contact, observes psychologist Elaine Ducharme, also matters. Is it steely or warm? Too much eye contact can be unnerving.

12. Handshake (not too firm, not too soft). Any businessperson can tell you the importance of a firm handshake in building confidence. However, like eye contact, there is a middle ground. Too firm suggests aggression; too soft suggests passivity.

Choice #6: Begin to Relate From My Own Sense of Personhood

Unhealthy vs. Healthy Attachement

A. Enmeshed

"I need you because love you." (Blind trust)
No individual identity. We depend upon others to determine acceptable/approved behavior. No internal motivation without input of others. We need to be carried.

B. Dependent

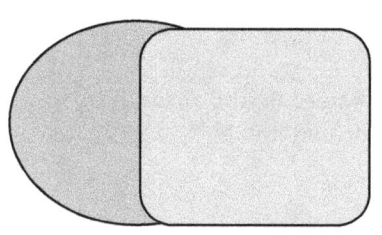

"I love you because I need you." (Dependent)
We are only able to pull away to become Individuals, when others give us permission to do so. Other people give us permission of whom to be. We allow other's opinions and attitudes to define our purpose. Our sense of self is derived from approval we receive.

C. Healthy Individuals

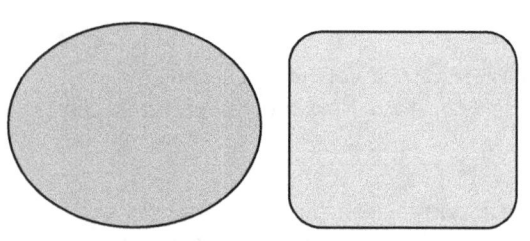

"I love you and I don't need you." (Individual)
We are each individuals, and would survive without the other. We each receive identity from our sense of relationship with God. This enables us to contribute to the relationship in a healthy manner.

Four Statements in the Healthy Apology

Healthy Apologies are essential in building Relationships

Note: A true apology is offered whether the other person is ready to reciprocate or not. Also, a true apology does not hold elements of, "I will if you will." When we repent to another person, we do so for the sake of the relationship, because we feel it is the right thing to do.

1. "I'm sorry."
We take ownership of our regret, and express our regret over our actions/words to the person who has experienced damaged relationship with us.

2. "I was wrong."
We acknowledge our lack of perfection, and communicate that we made a mistake in the relationship. To take this to its healthiest/deepest level, the "I was wrong statement" should also include the relational territory violated. For example: "I was wrong to speak to you that way," or "I was wrong to embarrass you in front of your friends."

3. "Would you please forgive me?"
We express our desire to continue the relationship, by requesting forgiveness. When we do, we realize that the other person is not immediately required to release us from the offense. In cases of deeper wounding, the ability to forgive might take time for the person to discover. If we try to apologize without forgiveness taking place, we short-circuit the relationship and make it totally one-sided; we avoid the real work of relating well – avoiding inevitable conflict. When we ask for forgiveness, it is a good practice to add the instance to the end of the question as well. Such as "Would you please forgive me for sending you that signal? I would never want to hurt you that way again, even unintentionally."

4. "What can I do to make things right between us?"
This statement sets a foundation for the healing work of restitution to take place. When we take ownership of our mistakes in relationship, seeking reconciliation and restoration, usually it will require a short period of re-building trust with the person we have injured. This process takes time, and effort.

Each of these four elements should be present in an apology, or a trust-gap will remain in the ability to relate.

Notes:

Situational Relationship Story

Karen works six days a week. She has two jobs, and has to schedule time to complete her family errands around her work schedule. She told a friend this week that she has to schedule time to take a shower. She feels very stressed over her job, and always deals with what psychologists call "time compression." She is a single-mother to two middle school children, and feels tremendous guilt for the time she spends away from them. Each week she has two nights available to spend with her children. She guards these evenings fiercely, and see them as her only opportunity to connect with them.

Karen's neighbor is an retired, widowed, elderly stay-at-home woman, who lives alone. Her name is Nancy. All of Nancy's children are grown, and have moved away. Although she lives alone, Nancy tries very hard to stay in contact with all of her neighbors. She is very vigilant about the safety of her neighborhood, and makes many telephone calls to the local police station with her concerns over cars she doesn't recognize, and joggers who look too long at her dining room window. Due to a bad hip, Nancy doesn't walk very well, and must exercise each day. She does this by walking slowly up and down the neighborhood road with her cane.

Each day, the time of Nancy returning to her home from her walk, seems to be the time when Karen is arriving home from her second job. Karen tries to avoid speaking with Nancy, because she doesn't want to become trapped in conversation. Karen feels desperate to spend time with her children, who are latch-key kids. She doesn't want to lose time with her children. When Nancy speaks to her, she refuses to answer, or makes her answers very short. Karen wants to be nice, but really feels bothered by what she has come to feel is Nancy's intrusion into her life.

Why do you think Karen has this life approach?

What elements of this relationship could be improved?

What do you think might happen?

The Journey Into Healthy Discipleship

Jesus said to His disciples, "If anyone desires to come after Me, let him deny himself and take up his cross and follow Me. For whoever desires to save his life will lose it, and whoever loses his life for My sake will find it." Matt 16:24-25

Level ONE – CLICHES – What the Word of God describes as the right life approach attitude when we live at this level in any of our relationships.
Philippians 2:3-4; Matthew 7:12; Luke 6:31; I Thessalonians 4:1-12; Matthew 5:20

Levels of Communication	Levels of Touch (Physical Bonding)	Levels of Mutual Relationship	Forms of Love	Human Needs Addressed	Father God's Attitude Toward Us
1. CLICHES (I.Q. – head) We experience Surface Appreciation and Admiration	1. Eye to Body (We talk "about") (We portray an "image" or "personage") (We have no accountability and we are unaware).	1. Attraction 2. Noticing Attributes 3. Appreciating Appearances We are Task/Performance Oriented	Phileo (friendship love) We represent Jesus and His character	To be praised To be seen (Our lives become about What is "normal" – fitting in.)	Jeremiah 29:11-13 Zephaniah 3:16-17

Level TWO – FACTS – What the Word of God describes as the right life approach attitude when we live at this level in any of our relationships.
Ephesians 6:7-8   I Corinthians 10:23-24   I Thessalonians 2:5-9   Psalm 119:91-120

Levels of Communication	Levels of Touch (Physical Bonding)	Levels of Mutual Relationship	Forms of Love	Human Needs Addressed	Father God's Attitude Toward Us
2. FACTS (I.Q. – head) We experience Common Interest and Discovery	2. Eye to Eye 3. Voice to Voice (We talk "to" others) (We portray an "image" or "personage, and now seek to gain approval) (Our relationships are based on conditional responses from others.)	1. Sharing Ideas 2. Light communication 3. Responding to trust We are Task/Performance Oriented	Phileo (friendship love) Storge (Caring Concern) We represent Jesus, His people, and His purposes.	To be seen To be safe To be included To be affirmed (Our lives become "surface" or "semi-surface," without depth.)	Isaiah 1:18 I Samuel 16:7 Psalm 103:2-5 Psalm 49:15 Numbers 12:6-8

Life on Levels 1 and 2 indicate the focus of a Carnal Believer — **Wall of Self-Protection** — **Life on Levels 3 and 4 indicate the focus of a Disciple**

Awakened!!

Level THREE – VALUES/FEELINGS/MORALS

What the Word of God describes as the right life approach attitude when we live at this level in any of our relationships.
I Corinthians 13   I Thessalonians 5   Matthew 5:38-48   Proverbs 11:3   Romans 13:8-14   I Corinthians 6:17-18

Levels of Communication 3. VALUES/FEELINGS & MORALS	Levels of Touch (Physical Bonding)	Levels of Mutual Relationship	Forms of Love	Human Needs Addressed	Father God's Attitude Toward Us
(E.Q. – heart)	1. Hand to hand	1. Active listening	Storge (Caring Concern)	To be touched	Lamentations 3:19-38
We experience Perception and true knowledge. We come into agreement with others and experience connection Discovery	2. Arm to Shoulder 3. Arm to waist (We talk "with" others) We portray a tentative expression of our real selves, testing ground for rejection). (Our relationships are based on mutual relationship and voluntary accountability.	2. Responsive trust 3. Loyalty 4. Sharing dreams And hopes We become Relationship Oriented	Agape (sacrificial love) We begin to realize our need to represent Jesus, and His nature.	To be heard To be belong To be received (Our lives become more aware of the needs and concerns of others.)	Jeremiah 33:3 Isaiah 59:1 Jeremiah 31:1-4

Level FOUR – NEEDS AND YEARNINGS

What the Word of God describes as the right life approach attitude when we live at this level in any of our relationships.
Psalm 51:6   I John 4   Ephesians 5:25-33   I Thessalonians 4:1-12   Proverbs 5:15-23   I Peter 1:13   II Corinthians 4:1-7   Hebrews 12:15   Ephesians 4:28-32

Levels of Communication 4. NEEDS and YEARNINGS	Levels of Touch (Physical Bonding)	Levels of Mutual Relationship	Forms of Love	Human Needs Addressed	Father God's Attitude Toward Us
(E.Q. – heart)	4. Face to Face 5. Hand to Head 6. Hand to Body (safe touch)	1. Freedom to choose to show real self	Agape (sacrificial love)	To be safe	Psalm 103:8-14
We experience Real Unity Discernment and Understanding	(We listen and share "with" others; we are real – congruent) – unspoken feit communication Voluntary Accountability and Discipleship	2. Emotional intimacy 3. Sharing fears and failures We are Relationship Oriented. We are authentic.	Eros (sexual love/chemical responses under control) We represent Jesus, and His Ministry and care	To be chosen To be understood To be included (Our lives become more aware of the needs and concerns of others.)	Psalm 119:117 Revelation 21:4 John 17

Level FIVE – MARRIAGE / CORE UNION
What the Word of God describes as the right life approach attitude when we live at this level in any of our relationships.

Psalm 51:6   1 John 4   Ephesians 5:25-33   1 Thessalonians 4:1-12   Proverbs 5:15-23   1 Peter 1:13

Levels of Communication	Levels of Touch (Physical Bonding)	Levels of Mutual Relationship	Forms of Love	Human Needs Addressed	Father God's Attitude Toward Us
5. MARRIAGE / CORE UNION (SPIRITUAL EMOTIONAL And PHYSICAL) IQ and EQ on both sides of the relationship. We experience Core bonded-ness Wisdom and safety	1. Mouth to body 2. Hand to genitals 3. Genitals to genitals (sexual union) (We share all of life's issues; past and present. We are naked and unashamed on all levels of the relationship.) *We are team minded and serving oriented*	1. Accepted without fear 2. Confident to trust 3. Emotionally vulnerable 4. Pro-active and mutual care; sacrificial expression without expectation or demand. We are Relationship Oriented. We are transparent.	*Agape (sacrificial love)* *Eros (sexual love)* We represent Jesus, and His Relationship to us.	To be safe To be chosen To be passionately desired (Our lives become focused upon serving and representing the Holy Spirit in our life actions, and in our words.)	John 15 Ephesians 5:25-26 Psalm 42:7

Notes:

This Week:

1. **Journal** *the discoveries you have made in the last two sessions, regarding your ability to relate to other people. Please take time to consider your answer from all angles.*

2. **Read** *chapters 1-4 of "Loving People" by John Townsend. If you are current in your reading, please use this time to go over discoveries you have made in the last three sessions. Make notes on the questions that rise as you read. .*

3. *At some point during the week, before the next class session, look over the journaling you have done over the past few sessions. What choices would you like to make in regard to changing your behavior patterns in relating to others? Make a list of areas where you would like to begin. Connect those areas with the unmet bonding needs we studied in the past few sessions.*

Session Seven – "What About Conflict and Negativity?"

What we will learn in this Session:

We will assess our personal discoveries so far, and begin the process of assessing where we are presently living in our ability to relate to others well. We will learn the difference between Judgment and Assessment, and discuss God's principle of Meditation/Agitation. We will learn in what ways all human beings are the same. We will learn how our inner thoughts regarding ourselves and others have affected our self-concept. We will utilize the materials disclosed so far to discover where we are in the Heart-Relational Ability- Recovery Process.

We will learn how Relationships Evolve, and see the pathway ahead. We will take a quick look at the study materials added to this session, regarding the inner road-blocks of Pride, Fear and Control, to aid the student in learning how to change their Inner Life orbit pattern, where needed. Finally, we will address possible missing puzzle pieces in our personal Life Experience history, and see what ingredients might be missing in our understanding of how healthy relationships/family work.

The Instructor's Goal for this Session:

To help the student begin the process of personalizing the materials studied so far. To open discussion for the class, for connection and discovery. To provide a safe environment where difficulties can be assessed without fear of judgment or disapproval.

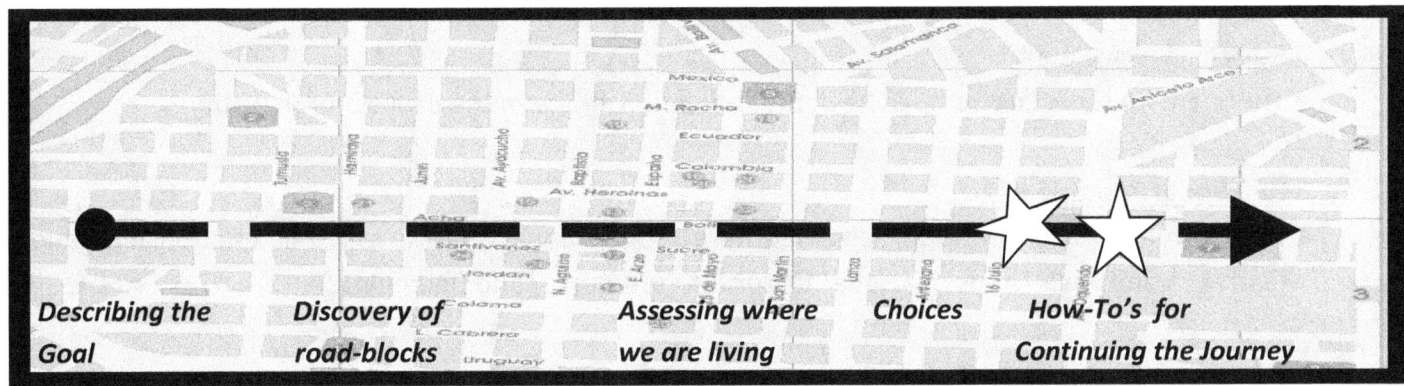

Session Seven

"What About Conflict and Negativity?"

Let's Review

Relational Principle #1 – Human beings are inherently self-centered, without ability or capacity to give or receive love outside of relationship with God, because <u>God is love</u>. Jesus Christ is God.

Relational Principle #2 – Spiritual development and emotional maturity are intricately connected and cannot be separated. Growth in these areas of life happens inter-dependently

Relational Principle #3 – Our experiences, imprintings and relationships in early life development are catalysts for our deep perceptions and core beliefs regarding ourselves and how life works. Elements that have hindered healthy living are destructive and must be addressed, owned and healed.

Relational Principle #4 – We cannot give away what we have never received.

Relational Principle #5 – When we become aware of our needs to bond, incremental choices and actions are required to begin/continue the connection/bonding process. Bonding does not "just happen."

Relational Principle #6 –
Connection, Bonded-ness and Attachment cannot be achieved without intentional pursuit. For the follower of Jesus Christ, this is a requirement for healthy discipleship and community (Body-Life).

Relational Principle #7 –
There are no short cuts to building depth in relationship or in the process of maturity

Relational Principle #8 –
Honest vulnerability with God, self and others is necessary in order to maintain relationships, and learn to bond well. This is the "glue" factor for Community and Belonging.

"Safe People Create Safe Places"

"Sometimes I just want to run Home."
"Make your home in Me as I make mine in you." (John 15:4).

> "Home is a place of welcoming love, nonjudgmental acceptance, kisses, and hospitality----elements that induce a profound sense of belonging"
> ....Brennan Manning.

Notes:

> **Relational Principle #9 –**
> **Some choices to grow will be made outside of personal emotion.**
> **Some choices to grow will be initially painful.**
> **New birth cannot happen without pain.**

Clue Question #31 (7) --
How important are your emotions to you when it comes to learning to relate to others? Are you willing to try to relate to others in a fresh and more healthy way, even if it is uncomfortable to you at first? What are the choices you see right now that you will need to make in your behavior patterns?

Let's take a little time to decipher what has broken down in past experiences in relationship.

The Cycle of Disaffection in Relationships

Bonding Gaps initiate a driven-ness to connect. Then, armed with an unhealthy understanding of how healthy relationships happen, we enter the cycle.

1. Search for Attachment/Bond
"I will find fulfillment."

2. Enamored
"This person is my fulfillment. I am safe. My needs are met."

3. Source Substitution
"I need no other relationships. This is a relationship bubble no one else can enter. I need this person to myself."

4. Conflict/Incompatibility
Bonding gaps feed the inability to build relationship.

5. Disillusionment
"The relationship isn't what I expected. I will wait with disappointment."

6. Anger in Hope – *"This is not right. My needs were met at one time... I will wait to see the behaviors from the beginning of the relationship."*

7. Negative communication
criticism, accusations, assumptions, contemptuous, defensiveness, retreat, silence, anger

8. Broken Trust/Withdrawal
"Behaviors have stolen my hope of fulfillment. This person is not safe. I am afraid to trust them."

9. Control & Fear *"I don't want to lose the relationship. I will create the fulfillment I need alone. I will be safe."*

10. Discarding of Relationship *"I cannot continue to do this alone.*

The cycle is fed by conflict, assumptions, and defense mechanisms

The cycle may be broken at any point, with the insertion and adherence to Truth, absent of self-defense mechanisms. The repair of the relationship happens first within each individual, in awareness, admission, and willingness to change.

© dg Awakened to Grow

The Downward Spiral of Dissolving a Relationship

When a relationship continues down the spiral, it begins to disintegrate. The downward slide requires no effort for the spiral to continue. However, the process of healing trust and developing community will require intentional effort.

The Ten Levels of the Staircase

1. **Established**—*Let's start a relationship*

2. **Ambushed** *The stresses of life set traps for conflict and disagreement*

3. **Anger** *Inability to resolve conflict ignites anger patterns*

4. **Fear** *Inner bully; we shut down*

5. **Isolation** *Each to their own station; we retreat and withdraw*

6. **Aloneness** *Waiting to be pursued; "if you love me you'll come after me."*

7. **Alienated** *"It's safer this way; I will find another way to feel significant."*

8. **Arrogance** *"I don't care what you think" "I have my own perceptions." "I've found what works for me – I don't need to change."*

9. **Adulteries of the Heart** *"Something else has my affection and loyalty." "I only want you when I have a need. Don't push your needs or express your heart to me."*

10. **Addictions & Loss of Relationship** *Stubborn blindness – "I need this, not you." "But don't leave me. I need you here for myself."*

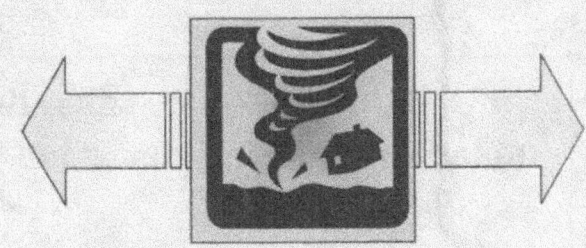

Clue Question #32 (7) –

How have past relationships experienced the descriptions provided in the past two charts? Looking back, what do you wish you had done differently in those situations?

What steps would you be willing to take now, given the same opportunity, to change the pathway of disaffection, or disintegration?

Are there choices you made that were healthy, and would have remained the same on your part? In what way?

Relational Principle #10 –
Relationships are maintained by a willingness to take risks in disclosure and trust.

Clue Question #33 (7) –

Considering all we have studied to date, how does the above Relational Principle apply in your ability to relate to others?

Situational Relationship Story

Heidi and David are high school sweethearts. Both of them have friendships at school and at church. Additionally, they both enjoy sports, especially football. It is all they can talk about.
When they aren't talking about football, they are cuddling up together on the couch, or sitting in the darkest parts of a movie theater.

David is 16. David's father is addicted to his job, and seldom home. His mother tries to smile and make the best of things, but refuses to allow conflict to become part of the atmosphere of the home. When David says, "I wish Dad had time to so _____," his mother chides him for not understanding the pressure his father is under, and for being critical of his father. She instructs him to develop a better attitude. David is afraid to speak with his father about what he feels, so he decides to just wait until he is old enough to escape and find a more loving environment for himself. In the midst of his loneliness and isolation, he discovers a website filled with pornographic materials. His physical reaction to the materials he has discovered, and his subsequent actions, become habitual. By the time he is 18, he has a secret functioning sexual addiction.

Heidi is 16. She has grown up in a privileged home, and has never had to do without anything. As a result, she carries a sense of entitlement. Her family is very close, and somewhat clannish in nature. There is one difficulty in her life, however, as she sees it. Her mother is a micro-manager who expects Heidi to perform as she is told, without argument. Heidi's grandmother has noticed that Heidi has become unhappy and stressed when she is around her mother in the past several years, and has offered to allow Heidi to move in with her, to get her away from the stresses she feels.

When Heidi is 18, and David is 19, they are alone one night on a date. Both of them have experienced difficulty at home, and are in need of comfort and relationship. Vulnerable, they disclose their home situations to each other. Emotions surface. They rent a motel room, and enter into a sexual relationship. This continues for several months. Afraid of rejection, David keeps his sexual addiction a secret.

Soon, they marry. Guilt-ridden, David discloses his addiction to his wife. She doesn't know what to do.

How will this relationship be affected by David's disclosure?
What are the crucial issues in this situation?
What common ground do you see?
What would you tell this couple?

> *"You can catch a cold, but you can't catch good health – it must be developed and maintained."*

Evidences of a Closed/Partially Closed Orbit in Relationship

1. The person is resistant to your ideas or counsel.
2. The person argues with your point of view.
3. They don't listen.
4. The want to be recognized as independent from you.
5. They don't want to be touched by you.
6. They avoid spending time in joint company.
7. They use disrespectful/unkind language with you.
8. They withdraw – either emotionally or physically.
9. They swear with they are angry.
10. They try to run away.
11. They try to commit suicide, or do self-harming actions.
12. They are unresponsive to affection or compliments.
13. . They seek friends opposite of your choice/ they "flip"
14. They say things like "I hate you," or "leave me alone."
15. They use drugs or alcohol, retreating into their behavior. (bondage vs. bonded-ness)

Evidences of Emotional Immaturity (Peter Pan)

1. The person is unaware/blind of other's station or situation.
2. It does not occur to them to operate with another person's interest at heart.
3. Self-centered. "Magical Thinking." "I am an exception."
4. Concrete thinker only. Can only relate to one instance at a time, rather than a pattern of behavior.
5. Makes statements, rather than asking questions.
6. Is unwilling to be wrong. Evasive conversation. Defensive.
7. Does not respond well to correction or conflict; pouts, whines, pushes for own way
8. Wants to be evaluated based on intentions rather than actions.
9. Reciprocates injuries. (Makes someone "pay.")
10. Will live on task level, and substitute physical connection for true emotional connection.

How to Reach "Peter Pan"
(Beginning places of earning/building Trust)

1. Intentionally become tender-hearted. Pray for them.
2. Stop arguing, and become gentle, even when you disagree.
3. Listen more. Increase your understanding of the person's emotions and perspectives.
4. Where you have wounded them, recognize and take ownership of the offense.
5. Be patient. The longer the season of wounding, the longer the season of rebuilding.
6. Attempt gentle, tentative touch (hand, arm; for connection only).
7. Use a soft and safe tone and level of voice.
8. Be consistent. Don't change.
9. Seek forgiveness.
10. Continue in this vein, until the person realizes that a change has taken place in you towards them. he person is unaware/blind of other's station or situation.

Tips: You can use emotional word pictures to help conversation. Gradual adjustment to this kind of change is necessary.

Pattern:
―――――――――――――――――――――――――――――――――▶

Comfort, light challenge, struggle, strategy, faith, tenacity, communication, back to comfort.

Notes:

This Week:

1. __Journal__ the discoveries you have made in the last two sessions, regarding your ability to relate to other people. Please take time to consider your answer from all angles. What new approaches are you putting to use in relationships from what you have learned? Write out your experiences.

2. __Read__ the remaining chapters of "Loving People" by John Townsend. If you are current in your reading, please use this time to go over discoveries you have made in the last three sessions. Make notes on the questions that rise as you read.

3. At some point during the week, before the next class session, look over the journaling you have done over the past few sessions. What choices would you like to make in regard to changing your behavior patterns in relating to others? Make a list of areas where you would like to begin. Connect those areas with the unmet bonding needs we studied in the past few sessions.

Session Eight – "Moving Forward"

What we will learn in this Session:

We will assess our personal discoveries so far, and discuss with practical application what we have gained during the past class sessions. We will address several relational situations as presented by the instructor, and discover together the how-to's of walking into deeper relationship. We will review questions and discoveries made, and reinforce our choices for steps we plan to take in relational living after the class is finished.

The Instructor's Goal for this Session:

To equip the student to continue in development of relational living after the class sessions are completed, and to help each student bring application to what they have learned.

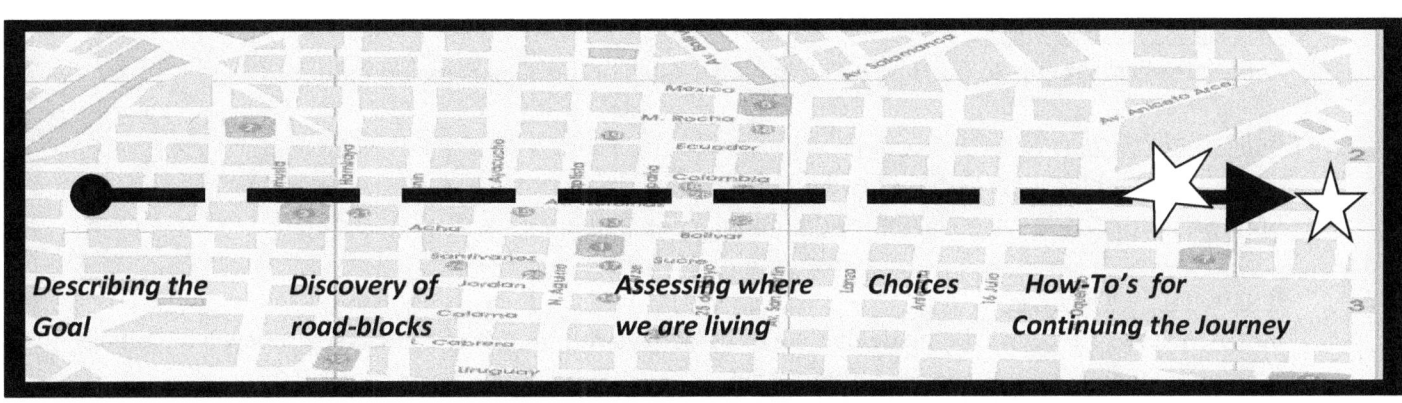

Session Eight
"Moving Forward"

Let's Review

Relational Principle #1 – Human beings are inherently self-centered, without ability or capacity to give or receive love outside of relationship with God, because <u>God is love</u>. Jesus Christ is God.

Relational Principle #2 – Spiritual development and emotional maturity are intricately connected and cannot be separated. Growth in these areas of life happens inter-dependently

Relational Principle #3 – Our experiences, imprintings and relationships in early life development are catalysts for our deep perceptions and core beliefs regarding ourselves and how life works. Elements that have hindered healthy living are destructive and must be addressed, owned and healed.

Relational Principle #4 – We cannot give away what we have never received.

Relational Principle #5 – When we become aware of our needs to bond, incremental choices and actions are required to begin/continue the connection/bonding process. Bonding does not "just happen."

Relational Principle #6 –
Connection, Bonded-ness and Attachment cannot be achieved without intentional pursuit. For the follower of Jesus Christ, this is a requirement for healthy discipleship and community (Body-Life).

Relational Principle #7 –
There are no short cuts to building depth in relationship or in the process of maturity

Relational Principle #8 –
Honest vulnerability with God, self and others is necessary in order to maintain relationships, and learn to bond well. This is the "glue" factor for Community and Belonging.

Relational Principle #9 –
Some choices to grow will be made outside of personal emotion. Some choices to grow will be initially painful. New birth cannot happen without pain.

Relational Principle #10 –
Relationships are maintained by a willingness to take risks in disclosure and trust.

"Simply Put"—for discussion-- 1

Relationships in the Garden of Eden showed Creation as the origination on Earth of the concept of Bonded-ness.

An allegiance or loyalty is a bond. When we substitute an allegiance before God, we become co-dependent, task-oriented, and fearful of man.

Our first allegiance, or loyalty is to God. We are called to move in obedience to His Holy Spirit's leading in our lives, based upon the Word of God.

Relational Situation #1

Catherine and John have been married for 10 years. They have both always felt they have a good marriage. Just before their seventh anniversary, Catherine's father, who was her childhood hero, passes away. At the same time, John receives a promotion at work, which changes his schedule and causes him to be gone for long hours, and sometimes for days on business trips.

Catherine begins to find herself dealing with feelings of isolation and abandonment. She finds she feels better when she keeps herself busy. She begins to spend money, finding comfort in shopping and pampering luxuries.

She doesn't tell her husband how she is feeling. He doesn't notice changes, and continues advancing in his job. Catherine begins to hide her spending from her husband, and takes out several credit cards he doesn't know about. For three years, she manages to hide her spending, and her husband doesn't notice, ask or communicate with her regarding her new clothes, or new items found around the house.

At the end of three years, Catherine finds herself unable to keep up with the interest payments on her secret cards. She has racked up over $75,000 in credit card spending.

How should she tell her husband?

How will he respond?

What will happen to this relationship?

"Simply Put"—for discussion-- 2

For a person with healthy bonding, an authority figure is a good thing.

Bonded people show the fruit of the Spirit in their relationships: Galatians 4:19

The elements of God's nature show themselves in His relationship with us. Our ability to do the right thing can only flow from our resting in His nature. We cannot show elements of His nature without relationship with Him.

Relational Situation #2

Charlie and Dan have been buddies for more than fifteen years. They have known each other since college days, when they met in the same fraternity house. Both graduated from college. Charlie went on to graduate school, and now serves as a consultant for a huge conglomerate. Dan went back home after college and began a hardware business in the small town he grew up in. The two men live about an hour from each other, and meet monthly to catch up over lunch together.

Charlie is very careful about his money, even though he is nearly a millionaire. Dan, on the other hand, has been hit hard by a difficult economy, and has had to down-size his family home in order to survive. Charlie collects, restores and drives antique cars, and muscle cars as his hobby. His latest rebuild, a bright red 1957 Chevy Bellaire, has a 500 horse-power racing engine, a specialty stereo system, and fully restored chrome detailing. Charlie paid $20,000 for just engine for his car.

Charlie drives the Bellaire, his latest rebuild, to the current monthly luncheon. Dan admires it and asks if Charlie would allow him to drive it. In a generous mood, Charlie offers to trade vehicles with his friend, and trade back at the next monthly luncheon.

Amazed and thrilled to have such a kind brother, Dan drives the collectible car home, and enjoys carefully driving it. Then, on his way to meet Charlie for lunch the next month, Dan gets in a hurry at a stoplight, and ends up rear-ending another driver at 35mph. The radiator is pushed into the engine, and the car stops running.

When Dan calls his friend to explain why he is late for their lunch together, Charlie assumes that Dan has driven the car recklessly for the entire past month.

How should this conflict be resolved?

What will be the key interests for each man?

Is there any middle ground in this conflict?

What will happen to this relationship?

Notes:

After the Class Concludes:

*1. Continue to **Journal** your discoveries regarding relationships. Frequently re-read your discoveries, allowing yourself to learn and grow. Remember to detach yourself from what you read in order to help yourself make objective observations.*

*2. Continue to **Read** in order to learn more about relationships and how they work. Here are some suggested reading offerings:*

"The DNA of Relationships"	Gary Smalley
"Love's Unseen Enemy"	Les Parrott
"High Maintenance Relationships"	Les Parrott
"Family Secrets"	John Bradshaw
"Connecting"	Larry Crabb
"The God Attachment"	Tim Clinton

If you enjoyed this curriculum, you might also enjoy:

"Elements of Identity Formation" also by Debbye Graafsma,d mcc, bcpc. This class discusses the believer's call to personal identity formation. For those who have experienced issues in developmental bonding, this class is essential for coming to a secure and confident place in living your life without pretensions, strong in Christ. (available on lulu.com)

"Journey: A Novel" by Debbye Graafsma. Based on more than 8 years of painstaking historical research, Debbye's novel on the life of Mary Magdalene presents a fresh and uniquely relational understanding of the healing, deliverance, and emotional development of the controversial woman whom Jesus delivered from demonic possession. This book is also one of the suggested reads for the "Elements of Identity Formation" class. (available on Amazon.com)

www.ingramcontent.com/pod-product-compliance
Lightning Source LLC
Chambersburg PA
CBHW080552230426
43663CB00015B/2809